It's My Party

a memoir

Jeannette Watson

TURTLE POINT PRESS

BROOKLYN, NEW YORK

Turtle Point Press
info@turtlepointpress.com

Library of Congress Cataloging-in-Publication Data is available from the publisher upon request

Book design by Phil Kovacevich

ISBN: 978-1-933527-99-4
ebook ISBN: 978-1-885983-50-3

Printed in the United States of America

For my beloved family:

my husband, Alex,

my three sons,

Ralph, Andrew, Matthew,

my daughter-in-law, Emily,

and my grandson, Henry

Last night I had a haunting dream about my father. I dreamed I was in an elderly friend's apartment, waiting for her, when suddenly a closet door opened in front of me and out walked my father: not my old father, now deceased, but my young father, from when I was a little girl...I was terrified at first, but then noticed how lost he looked, gliding past me as though he didn't see me. I said, "Daddy can I help you? How are you?" At which point I woke up, heart pounding, and tried to sort out my feelings.

Chapter One

I have always loved to laugh: a loud, raucous belly laugh, which, I regret to say, often ends in a snort. My father felt my laugh was unfeminine. He used to say, "With a laugh like that you'll *never* find a husband!" Years later I would tease him, saying, "I was able to find not just one, but two, in spite of my laugh." Actually, my first husband hated my laugh, but so far — thirty-seven years — Alex, my second husband, doesn't seem to mind it.

My parents' first baby, Thomas J. Watson III, died as a baby, just before Christmas in 1942. I can imagine how devastating it must have been for a young couple to lose their first child. The baby died without warning, of no known cause. Their second son, my brother Tom, arrived two years later. (I would later think it quite weird that they gave the second baby the same dynastic name as the first, as though the first baby hadn't existed.) I was born sixteen months after that, on October 9, 1945, and then came Olive, Lucinda, Susan, and Helen. The first four of us were bunched within six years of each other, with the last two girls born in the next six. My parents had hoped for another boy but gave up after five girls.

Taking care of six children was quite an undertaking, especially because my mother was also a corporate wife who had to travel and attend business functions with my father. A baby nurse cared for us in our first six months, before we graduated to the care of a governess. When I was about three, my parents decided an English governess would be just the ticket for us, and off to London they went to find "the perfect nanny." My mother spent the morning at an agency interviewing

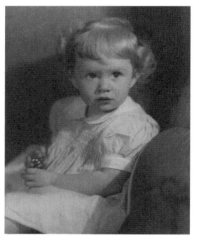

TOP: Olive with Tom and six-month-old Jeannette

BOTTOM: Jeannette looking pensive at age one

candidates. She narrowed them down to two. She told my father that one was pretty, and one had dyed red hair and bad breath. My father told her to hire the second one, on the theory that she would never marry and could devote her life to raising us.

Nana, or "Nanner" as we children called her, did not have an easy life with us in Connecticut. Back then nannies were on call twenty-four hours a day and were only off on Thursdays and Sunday afternoons. Nana had a small room where

Lucinda, Jeannette, and Olive in the "pram"

she kept her meager life possessions and her African violets. On prominent display was a photo of the previous child she had cared for, the saintly Nicholas. She always referred to him as her *dee-ee-ar* Nicholas. We, sadly, were neither saintly nor dear. My mother often countermanded Nana's edicts, undercutting her authority and implicitly condoning disrespectful behavior from us. I often felt extremely guilty at my rudeness when I saw Nana go weeping to her room. She stayed with our family for almost ten years. None of us kept in touch with her after she left. I knew other children had very close relationships with their nannies, and my husband, Alex, adored Joannie, his nanny, but I don't recall any affection between Nanner and me.

Nana brought a British vocabulary with her that became our own. A washcloth was a "flannel." "Woolies" were the horrible pink long underwear we girls were forced to wear over our underpants. (They were made of scratchy wool and came down almost to our knees. We all hated them and lived in terror that a classmate at school might see them.) A "windy-pop" was a somewhat endearing name for a fart. When one of us misbehaved, which was often, she would say, "Beg [pronounced *baaaaayg*] pardon," as if she were speaking to an errant dog.

Nana took a special interest in our bowels. Clockwork regularity was the goal, and every Thursday afternoon we had little glasses of prune juice. Her term for a bowel movement was "big job," and when we went to the bathroom, Nana asked, "Big job or little job?" I remember she made us all sit on different

The pony cart we used to collect blackberries

toilets every morning to do our business, and when we finished, we would give the assigned signal from our various command posts: "Nanner — I'm all readyyyy." After her inspection we were allowed to leave the toilets.

~

When we first moved to Meadowcroft Lane in Greenwich, it was quite bucolic. There was still a lot of open land and even some working farms. We had lived in two other houses in Greenwich prior to Meadowcroft, but I was too young to remember them. The end of the lane was filled with blackberry bushes, and we had a little pony that would pull us in a cart so that we could go exploring and collect blackberries.

Every day Nana would lead us on a long walk, pushing the latest baby in a carriage, which she called the "pram." We would walk from Meadowcroft Lane, turn right on Greyhampton Lane, go down the hill to Lake Avenue, and then make a left toward the green bench (called "the form" by Nana), where we would gaze at the herd of cows that have long since been displaced by houses. After a brief rest on the form we would march home.

With so many children around, something was always happening to one of us — falls, concussions, sprains, and scrapes were commonplace. We also seemed to injure each other during unsupervised "play." My parents felt that we had to deal with our own battles and did not encourage us to tattle. Luckily during active warfare I could run faster than some of them and would race upstairs and lock myself in my bathroom and read the books I kept there. We had strong feelings about each other, sometimes verging on the murderous, but pencil stabbings were as close as we came to sororicide. Sometimes I prayed that some of my siblings would be painlessly and miraculously removed from the family. After praying for this ardently for several months I gradually lost my faith, but I dutifully recited our scary nighttime prayer:

> Now I lay me down to sleep
> I pray the lord my soul to keep
> If I should die before I wake
> I pray the lord my soul to take

Sleep and death became intertwined, causing nightmares.

Our house was a fairly conventional white-washed brick. The brick color came through the paint, giving it a slightly pink hue. The front door opened onto a spacious entryway. To the left a gracious curving stairway led to the second floor. In a niche under the staircase stood a table where the mail and magazines were placed. There was a third floor, not visible from the first floor. The main residence eventually had eight bedrooms: one for my parents, one for the nanny, and one for each child. As new babies arrived we were shuffled around. Eventually Olive and I, as the two oldest girls, moved to the third floor. At first we slept in one large room, where my numerous dolls lived in their own tiny room in a corner. I had a Ginger Doll with her own trunk filled with beautiful clothes. Another doll came with a lovely canopied bed. I remember a Betsy Wetsy, to whom I fed water, causing her to wet her diaper, which I changed. I must have had at least thirty dolls: baby dolls and dolls appearing to be anywhere from four to ten years old, all different sizes. This was before the age of Barbie, so I didn't have any sexy teenage dolls. My dolls were beautiful and would be collector's items now. I spent hours caring for them.

Olive and I used to discuss which bed in our room was safer. I slept next to the door and felt a robber would get me first. Olive said a ghost coming out of the closet would get to her before it got to me. Later on, my parents felt we should each have our own rooms, so two bedrooms were created, with a large bathroom.

I was happy to have my own room, where I could disappear and read, and a bathroom door that I could lock in case I was in need of a retreat from a battle with one of my siblings. I always kept the bathroom supplied with books, though I can't remember where I got them all. I do know that in the early days we went to the library, and later on I think I just read whatever I found around the house—often *Reader's Digest* condensed novels.

There were enormous attics off our hallway, one of which was filled with my brother's elaborate electric train set. Another was used to hang some of my mother's dresses. I remember in particular a bright-red flamenco dancer's dress edged in white lace with a black-fringed shawl. In later years it was joined by a strapless floral ball gown with a note attached, in my mother's handwriting: "Worn at the White House dinner seated next to Jack Kennedy." My sister Olive said she also saw the dress my mother wore when she was Peanut Queen at some festival long ago: It was a form-fitting V-neck long dress covered entirely with peanut shells. My deb party dresses joined my mother's dresses in the long attic.

Downstairs, branching off and to the right of the front hall, carpeted wall-to-wall in pale green, was the wood-paneled library, where we would welcome my father when he returned from work, usually around 6:30. "Get down to the library!" Mummy would command. "Your father is coming home!" He arrived like a general intent on conducting a full-dress review of his regiment. As he wrote in his autobiography, "I often ended up carrying my frustrations home with me, where my wife and children would bear the brunt. Olive would spend the entire day working with them, and she'd have them all shined up and ready to greet me when I came home. I'd come in the door and say, 'That child's sock isn't pulled up. That child's hair isn't combed. What are these boxes doing in the hall? They should have been mailed.' It was the same demanding IBM attitude, and it was very hard on them all."

The library was also the place where we were summoned for scoldings if we had misbehaved or fallen short at school. These "Library Lectures" could be quite stern, even harsh, and some of the things my father said left permanent bruises. Fortunately, I mostly managed to stay off the radar. I rarely did anything good, but I rarely did anything bad either.

Just off the library was a formal living room that we never used. Its furniture was dark, and its sofas were stiff and uncomfortable. Beyond the living room was a screened-in porch. This porch became known as the "poor room," as my two younger sisters wanted a place where they could entertain their friends in a more casual way, without being embarrassed by the "rich" look of the rest of the house.

To the left of the front hall stood the very austere formal dining room, with dark polished wood floors under an oriental rug. The room was dominated by a large mahogany table, which could be made even bigger with the insertion of more leaves. On the sideboard the obligatory silver tea service reigned in stately splendor alongside a black lacquered Chinese screen.

The dining room led into the less formal "breakfast room," where we sat at a round table featuring a lazy Susan designed by my father to efficiently pass the sugar, cereal, butter, and jam. During the week we had a quick breakfast—I usually ate Grape Nuts with bacon crumbled on top. But weekends were different: eggs on Saturday and waffles Sunday.

The breakfast room was just off the pantry, with its glass-door cabinets filled with Steuben glass and sets of china. Adjacent to the pantry was a large kitchen with a double sink and several ovens. The "help" had a small sitting room off the kitchen with a sofa and two chairs for watching TV. A narrow staircase led up to the "servants' wing," which had two bathrooms and four small bedrooms: for the autocratic Russian cook Willie and his German, stereotypically-Nazi-like wife Mary, who was our housekeeper and waitress, and for Hannelori, Mary's pretty, somewhat sexy, buxom young German assistant. Hannelori wore form-fitting uniforms, unbuttoned one button lower than usual, and large fake dangly diamond earrings. She created quite a sensation, in general. We were rarely allowed in this part of the house because Willie and Mary disliked children. Nanner slept upstairs in a room between my two younger sisters. A laundress came several days a week to labor in the Stygian inferno of our large, dark basement, and on Thursdays, which was the cook's and nannie's night off, a lovely Irish woman named Margaret came to take care of us. On those nights we were allowed to make our own delicious sandwiches—Skippy peanut butter and Smucker's raspberry jam on Wonder Bread. I had eggnog with my supper (no alcohol!), which I mixed up in the blender.

After Margaret had sandwiches with us, my mother cooked dinner for my father. I remember thinking how *dull* his dinner was: a hamburger and baked potato, with frozen vegetables, served to him by my mother on a tray in the library.

We had what in the '50s might have been considered a large house (though not unusually so for Greenwich). Two years ago I took my son Matthew to see the place where I grew up. I was horrified to see that Meadowcroft Lane is now chock-a-block with McMansions three and four times bigger than my old house and built on plots significantly smaller. My sister Susan recently sent me a Sotheby's description with photos of our house, which was for sale. It had practically doubled in size, with elaborate servants' quarters. I could scarcely recognize it.

We lived on about seven acres of land perched on a hill above a lake. Along the hill were flower beds, where a full-time gardener seemed to plant mainly roses. A small ornamental pond filled with goldfish sat nestled in a group of trees, with a large open fire pit nearby for barbecues.

Our lake was a source of great pleasure. Several majestic weeping willow trees sheltered our small dock. We had a canoe that we loved taking out on the water. A strip of land separated our lake from another one that had two small islands. We could drag the canoe across to explore the other lake and its little islands.

In the winter the lake froze over, and gliding over its black ice was the best time I ever had on skates. Sometimes my parents had cookouts by the lake, with hamburgers and hot cocoa to warm us up. When I was four and my brother six we were wandering unattended by the lake. He told me to avoid a place where the ice was thin, a warning that I blithely ignored. The ice broke, and suddenly I was in the cold dark water. Luckily for me, my brother was able to pull me out, and we went back home. I remember my mother taking off all my wet clothes in the kitchen (much to my humiliation) and then marching me upstairs to a warm bath. No one seemed too concerned: perhaps because there were so many of us!

In warm weather we roamed around the neighborhood without supervision. We each had our own "fort"—some hidden spot under a tree or behind a bush that was filled with "ammunition" (stones with which to attack our other siblings). After tiring of our own property, we explored old graveyards and vast estates. Local kids would gather at our house and we girls would play jump rope for hours, chanting:

> Down in the meadows where the green grass grows
> There sits (some girl) pretty as a rose
> Along came (some boy) and kissed her on the nose
> How many kisses did she receive?

Then we counted, the rope accelerating as the numbers rose, until the jumper missed a beat. We also played hopscotch, enacted scenes as Roy Rogers and Dale

Evans, and invented dances. On rainy days we played jacks, pick-up sticks, and built houses out of playing cards. How innocent it all seems.

Our father gave Olive and me a little electric car that we shared—on the back it said "Jeannette odd days, Olive even days," so we wouldn't fight. Later on, we started skateboarding and used to drive to a nearby deserted house, a replica of Le Petit Trianon, whose long, sloping driveway was perfect for our new sport.

We had a little red playhouse with a real kitchen, where I would bake "answer cakes" (named after the mix it came in), which I embellished with chocolate frosting from a can. Sometimes we spent the night there. A tennis court stretched out beyond the playhouse, but we rarely used it.

We always seemed to have a large number of pets, and my parents were quite tolerant of them. The first pet I remember was Sambo, a huge Newfoundland. He was the sweetest dog and uncomplainingly let us ride on his back or do anything else we wanted. We all adored him, although I think our parents were vexed by the havoc he caused. Anytime a door in the house was left open, he would happily bound through the screen, totally destroying it.

Around this time, my grandmother Watson gave me a cat that I called Little Nipper—for obvious reasons. The two pets became inseparable: Nipper curled up next to Sambo, serving as a tiny pillow. When Nipper was injured and later put down, Sambo was inconsolable. In those days, if anything was wrong with a pet it was usually euthanized. There were no elaborate (and expensive) surgeries, medications, or acupuncture treatments. Later on I got a Mexican Chihuahua called Mitzy, whom I trained to sit, shake hands, and walk on her hind legs. I often dressed her up in doll clothes.

We had two golden retrievers: Punch, who belonged to Tom, and Mark, who became Olive's. Punch was wonderfully gentle, and I loved him. Lucinda had a basset hound named Maynard, and of course various gerbils and goldfish came and went.

When one of the dogs killed a mother rabbit, I raised the babies in my room, nestling them in a cardboard box and feeding them from a tiny eyedropper. We later released them in hopes they would find some relatives on our property.

I often think of the food from my childhood. It was classic '50s fare. I remember the soft comforting taste of Pablum, warm and sweet, and red Jell-O, which had a slippery consistency but no taste. I especially liked tapioca, a light dessert that was white and creamy with little chewy spots. We always added a spoonful of strawberry jam to white junket, smooth and soft. Custard was another bland, creamy favorite.

I grew up at a time when frozen food was becoming popular. How I loved Birds Eye beef pie, which was sometimes served on Sunday nights, when the cook was off. On Fridays we ate hamburgers and French fries with buttery Birds Eye frozen corn. We also enjoyed TV dinners, with each item confined to its own little compartment.

My parents worried a lot over bad breath and were constantly blaming garlic as the main cause of it—also raw onions, which I quite liked. At one point my mother said sweetly to me, "I hope you don't mind my telling you this, but your breath is *fetid*." When she saw my face fall she said, "Oh, do you mind my telling you? I'm always <u>thrilled</u> when your father tells me." (I would imagine the conversation. My father: "Olive, your breath is fetid!" My mother, gratefully: "Oh Tom, thank you so much for telling me!")

Because of their strong feelings about garlic, our meals were quite bland. Our father did make a delicious spaghetti sauce (without garlic) a few times a year, usually when we were in our home in Vermont. He enjoyed shopping for his ingredients and creating his sauce.

As children, the six of us were reluctant to try anything new. One night we were served apple Brown Betty with hard sauce, which we initially refused to taste. Our father insisted, and ultimately we all liked it.

We also protested when my father had the cook switch from butter to margarine, on his doctor's recommendation. Daddy asserted that we couldn't tell the difference and had us wear a blindfold as he gave us the test: toast with butter or toast with margarine? Olive could always tell immediately.

When we were little, we ate in the "children's dining room." One by one, as each of us turned eight, we moved to the "grown-up dining room," where the atmosphere was much more formal and good manners were required (sitting up straight, not speaking with one's mouth full, etc.). Often my father, still be in executive mode from work, spent dinner interrogating my mother:

"Olive, have you written that thank-you note to the Thornes?" he said strictly.

"Oh Tom," (hand raised to mouth, eyes wide) she said abjectly. "I'm so sorry, I forgot."

"How could you forget? We discussed it this morning!" he would snap.

Sometimes I wondered if she "forgot" on purpose, because this happened so often. It was like watching Martha and George go at it in *Who's Afraid of Virginia Woolf?* The sharp volleys of my parents' conversation could be quite exciting, but mostly they were gut-wrenching, especially when my father lost his temper. "The kids would scatter like quail," he wrote, "and Olive would catch the brunt of my frustration." Sometimes she would run upstairs and he would run after her.

My mother, a former model, was concerned about our looks and particularly our weight. Being "attractive" was very important to both my parents. At one point Daddy remarked on our "porkiness." We were very devoted to our cook Willie's chocolate chip cookies, especially warm from the oven. My parents decided this was contributing to the problem, so they kept the cookies locked up. When we sought them out, Willie's wife Mary would say, in her guttural, harshly-accented voice, "No, you may *not haff* cookies — your mother says you are *too* fat."

The emphasis on whether people were attractive bothered me. My mother sometimes passed the time playing the "Attractive Game." She'd point to two people and ask who was the most attractive. I naturally played along, but not happily, because I was so insecure about my own looks. I have struggled my whole life to shake the impulse to judge people by their looks. I'll be sitting in the subway and I'll think to myself, "Oh, that woman is so fat." Then I say to myself, "Don't look at her that way, look how she's holding her child, think something nice about her." It's gotten to the point that I hate the word "attractive."

After dinner, if I wasn't too porky, I would sit in front of the TV alongside some of my siblings with warm chocolate chip cookies and a glass of cold milk, gazing at my crush Edd "Kookie" Byrnes as he combed his pompadour on *77 Sunset Strip*, or else admiring the beautiful Gardner McKay in *Adventures in Paradise*. Years later I was thrilled to become friends with Nick Dunne, the best-selling author who'd produced the show. Someday I'll have to watch it again and see if it has retained its old allure. I'm sure Gardner McKay will be as gorgeous as ever.

Watching television was a great treat because my father considered it "the instrument of the devil." I remember as a little girl thinking the people inside the TV could see me, and being embarrassed if I had my bathrobe on. When I was around five, my father somehow arranged for Tom and me to appear in the peanut gallery of *The Howdy Doody Show*. I remember Buffalo Bob yelling at the rowdy children, then instantly adopting his affable TV persona when the cameras rolled.

My father, mother, and four kids (from left, Olive, me, Tom, and Lucinda) in one of
my father's antique cars

On Sundays we all went to church — first to the simple white Congregational Church on Round Hill Road, which I loved, and later to the more social and formal Episcopal Church, which I felt no connection to. After church we would come home and eat a served lunch in our Sunday clothes. We would have roast beef or lamb, gravy, roast potatoes, and frozen green beans or peas or corn. For dessert, there was always a special treat for the children, like ice cream with chocolate sauce.

On Sunday afternoons we would go on long family bike rides up and down the steep hills of Greenwich. I lived in terror that someone from my school, Greenwich Country Day, would see me doing something so dorky as riding bikes with my family. Now I think it was sweet that my parents wanted to spend so much time with us.

If we weren't bike-riding, Daddy might take us on a drive to see friends. I remember visiting Sam Pryor, former head of Pan Am. He had a huge collection of dolls from all over the world, and even asked his friends Gene Tunney and Charles Lindbergh to look for interesting dolls on their travels. The collection eventually grew to eight thousand dolls — the most valuable doll collection in the world. We also visited James Melton, who, like my father, was an antique-car enthusiast with

The first *Palawan* off the Maine coast

a large collection. He was extremely handsome, and I had something of a crush on him. A popular singer in the '20s and '30s, he made his Metropolitan Opera debut as Tamino in Mozart's *The Magic Flute*. Winthrop Rockefeller later bought most of his car collection, and some of it ended up in a museum in Seal Cove, Maine.

My mother used to take us to Tod's Point to swim and have a picnic on the beach. We had yummy sandwiches and hard-boiled eggs, usually followed by green grapes, and, if we were lucky, those sinful chocolate chip cookies.

Our salads were made with iceberg lettuce — the only kind of lettuce I knew. Years later, after my divorce and my move back to New York City, I rented a house in East Hampton with a friend who was a wonderful cook. We drove to the Green Thumb to buy our vegetables, and my job was to get the salad ingredients. When I returned triumphantly with the iceberg lettuce she was horrified, and opened my eyes to other possibilities. My mother served iceberg lettuce at her cookouts until she died. My husband, Alex, who loves iceberg lettuce, was always grateful.

In the summer, we went cruising off Maine in my father's fifty-one-foot sloop, *Palawan..* We stopped frequently at the islands that dot the coast. To cook hamburgers, we'd often place our patties on stones heated in a wood fire. We loved exploring these rocky islands and picking wild blueberries — and also bringing back

Jeannette at sea, with *Mary Poppins* and donuts

messy bouquets of wild flowers for my mother. As it grew dark my father and other grownups would tell spine-tingling ghost stories by the flickering fire — stories that sometimes gave us nightmares. Sometimes, my father would create a path out of pieces of a torn-up newspaper, a "paper chase" leading to a pile of candies.

I gladly participated in all of these activities, but my happiest hours were spent reading. When I wasn't immersed in a book, I often felt sad, lonely, and inadequate. All of my siblings seemed more at ease, more athletic, and more popular than I was. I felt I couldn't share my feelings with my parents, as they thought if I wasn't happy it was my own fault. I guess I was experiencing the first signs of the depression that would plague me for so much of my life, but I had no way of knowing that at the time. Books transported me to sunnier places and became an addiction as powerful as alcohol or drugs. Marcel Proust said, "There are perhaps no days of our childhood we lived so fully as those we spent with a favorite book." This was especially true for me. I vastly preferred the world of my books to the life I was living.

Chapter Two

My grandfather and grandmother, Thomas and Jeannette Watson, lived in a double townhouse at 4 East Seventy-Fifth Street, between Madison and Fifth. My grandfather bought the fifty-foot-wide mansion in 1939 from Stanley Mortimer, an heir to the Standard Oil of California fortune and a descendant of John Jay, the first chief justice of the U.S. Supreme Court. The house was built in 1896 for the McReady family and designed by Trowbridge, Colt and Livingston in the French Renaissance style. The McReadys lived there with seven servants. When Mortimer bought the house, he put in a bronze gate designed by Carrère and Hastings. In 2006, the house was sold for $53 million, at the time the highest price ever paid for a Manhattan townhouse.

My grandfather was a self-made man, the personification of the American dream. He was born in a small house in Painted Post, New York, to parents newly emigrated from Ireland, to avoid the potato famine, but originally from Scotland. One time my father visited the Watson homestead and found the house being rebuilt after a fire. Daddy said to the workmen, "I didn't know my father grew up in a house as nice as this." One of them said, "Hell no—this is much bigger than his house. It's the house he would have liked to have grown up in."

Grandfather attended a one-room schoolhouse and later, for a short time, a business school. One of his early jobs involved selling musical instruments from a horse and buggy. One day, while at work, he saw a bar, tied up his horse, and got drunk. On leaving the bar, he saw that his buggy had been stolen, along with the musical instruments. He vowed not to drink again and amazingly kept his vow. Much to the dismay of their guests, my grandparents served only one small glass of wine before dinner at their parties. After that, it was cold turkey!

In fact, my grandparents met at a dinner party, where my grandfather looked down the table and saw that my future grandmother was the only other person not drinking. (I feel I would have been biased the other way if I noticed a man not drinking!)

After an undistinguished early career, he started flourishing while working for the National Cash Register Company in Dayton, Ohio, where he met and married my grandmother. My grandfather and thirty-eight other NCR employees were accused of unfair business practices and were tried and convicted. He appealed, and the case was dropped. Grandfather argued with the top executive John Henry Patterson and was fired at age forty, just as he married my grandmother.

He came to New York, penniless, to look for work. My father told me that my grandfather, in order to present a good front and impress any employer, hired a limousine to take him to his interviews. Ultimately he was hired by an obscure company, the Computing-Tabulating-Recording Company, and became the driving force behind its transformation into IBM.

Grandfather literally went from rags to riches. At one point he'd owned only one suit and had to wrap himself in newspapers while waiting for it to be cleaned. By the time I knew him, he looked very distinguished, always formally dressed in three-piece suits made by Henry Poole of Savile Row, Winston Churchill's tailor. In the summer, he wore white suits and a Panama hat with a broad brim. Years later, on a trip to London with Alex, a man at Poole's showed me the records of my grandfather's suits. My father, who had his clothes made at Chipp in New York, never matched his elegance.

Grandfather became general manager of Computing-Tabulating-Recording (CTR) Company in 1914, the year my father was born, and its president in 1915, when he was forty-one years old. My grandfather has been called "the world's greatest salesman," and he was among the first to create a distinct corporate culture. His salesmen dressed in suits, ties, and white shirts, giving them more self-respect and a greater ability to connect with their customers. As children we often mocked the inspirational slogan THINK. We used to sing "T H I N K spells think: that's our family motto." IBM had its own symphony, country club, and songbook. In 1936, my grandfather amazingly earned the highest salary in America — $365,000, which would be around $6 million today.

As one of the highest-paid men in America, it seemed fitting that my grandfather raised his family in the wealthy suburb of Short Hills, New Jersey. My father remembers that some of the neighboring families considered the Watsons to be "nouveau," and they were often excluded from the more "exclusive" parties. This probably accounts for my grandfather's determination to see his family rise in society. I wonder what his old neighbors in Short Hills thought when my grandfather became FDR's man in New York, entertaining heads of state and royalty. I heard that, because of all the IBM stock he acquired, my grandfather's chauffeur became one of the richest men in Sweden when he retired there.

I loved spending the night at my grandparents' house in the city. My mother would drop me off and, suddenly, instead of being part of a big family, I was an adored only child. When I came up the big marble staircase to the third floor, where the bedrooms were, I turned to the left, toward the street-side of the house. At the end of a long hallway were two bedrooms, one on each side of the hall. To the left was my grandparents' bedroom, with bathroom. They slept in a double bed. Across from my grandparents' room was another large bedroom with twin beds, which was where I slept. I felt the energy of the city when I heard street noises outside as I was going to sleep.

A large formal portrait of my grandparents' four children hung on the wall of "my" bedroom. There was also a television, and often we would watch a program (sometimes *Lassie*) as we ate our dinner. Tables would be set up in front of each of us for our dinner trays. (The townhouse was later owned by the arts patron Rebekah Harkness, and, ironically enough, a real estate agent asked me, years later, if I would like to buy it for Books & Co.)

My grandfather called me his "Precious Promise," perhaps because I was the oldest female grandchild. When I stayed with him in New York, we would often spend mornings walking to Central Park to feed the ducks or watch the boats racing near the Hans Christian Andersen statue. Sometimes we went on horse-and-buggy rides, and I got to sit up front, next to the driver, and occasionally took the reins. Other times, my grandfather would take me into a toy store and tell me the happiest words a child can imagine: "What would you like? I'll get you anything you want." I always wanted a doll.

My grandfather with his "Precious Promise"

When I was about three, my grandfather took me on a business trip with him, just the two of us. We went to Poughkeepsie so that he could check out an IBM plant. I remember sleeping in the same bed and feeling happy and secure. Years later, when I went to my father's retirement party, an ancient woman approached me and identified herself as my grandfather's secretary and she said "I remember your grandfather asked me to give you a bath." I can't imagine a CEO of today asking his secretary to bathe his grandchild.

I never felt the same unselfconscious love of my father. I felt awkward just holding his hand. It was completely different with my grandfather. He wasn't scary, he wasn't going to scream at me, he just loved me. I could sit in his lap in a way that I never could with my father. I felt totally adored.

Daddy describes his tumultuous relationship with his father in his autobiography, which I recently reread and found far more revealing than I had previously realized. "From very early in life," my father admitted in the first chapter, "I was convinced that I had something missing. I was never able to connect with what other people were doing." I was shocked to read: "Father [my grandfather] must

Visiting Grandfather at IBM

have known he had an uncontrollable temper that might feed on itself, because when there was punishing to be done, he made Mother do it...I would go up to their white-tiled bathroom. Father would stand near the basin to observe, I would hold onto a towel rack, and Mother would do the switching."

It is painful in every sense to imagine this ritual, and it also seems weird that my grandfather would stand by as spectator. I can only imagine that these switchings had a devastating effect on my father and possibly increased his feelings of anger as an adult.

As a grownup, I could never reconcile this gentle man with the harsh taskmaster who had such a fraught relationship with my father. The switching of my father seemed so out of character, as did my grandfather's harsh words to him when he was a boy and later at IBM. Both of them had explosive tempers, and their frequent fights at work would often end in tears. I suppose they had become

In front of the Thomas J. Watson Library at the Metropolitan Museum of Art
(photo by Joyce Ravid)

rivals of sorts at IBM, with my grandfather wanting to stay in charge and my father impatient to take over.

For all of us grandchildren, the townhouse was like a palace, with marble floors and a huge winding staircase. Near the staircase was a tiny jewel-like elevator with a red-velvet interior and a tiny plush velvet bench. We loved playing in it and rode up and down endlessly. I remember a large, dark living room where sometimes the grandchildren would sit on the floor while Grandfather showed us a painting. I remember in particular a depiction of a Western landscape, where all the cows were encircled by bulls to protect them from marauding Indians.

He gave my parents a Monet for their wedding present and was an early collector of Grandma Moses. He became a patron of the arts, and the Salmagundi Club, founded in 1871 as a gathering place for artists and collectors, honored him with a dinner on his seventieth birthday. The boy from Painted Post was on a membership roll that at one time or another included William Merritt Chase, Charles Dana Gibson, Childe Hassam, Norman Rockwell, Augustus Saint-Gaudens, Stanford White, and N.C. Wyeth.

As a flower girl at my Aunt Jane's wedding

My grandfather used to amaze me with his "tricks." He had very strong hands and could crack a walnut with them; I would then get to pick out the delicious meat inside. He had dentures on the side of his mouth, and I can remember him making those teeth disappear and reappear, which I thought was nothing short of miraculous.

I have a weakness for beautiful clothes, and it was my beloved grandfather who put me on the road to perdition. He brought me exquisite coats, bonnets, and dresses from Paris. One year for Christmas he gave me a white ermine muff, which sent me over the moon.

The first dress I remember was the one I wore as a flower girl in my aunt Jane's wedding. It was long and pink, with a flowered pink organdy overlay and a pink satin sash. The ensemble was completed with pale pink slippers and a small dainty bouquet of tiny pink and white flowers. I felt like a princess. I remember waiting to walk down the aisle, gazing at my aunt Jane in her lovely dress, saying somewhat too loudly, "Aunt Jane, you look so beautiful!"

I have such sharp memories of my grandfather that my granny seems pale by comparison. She looked like a storybook grandmother (which no one does anymore), with white hair in a kind of twist at the back. She was partial to somewhat shapeless dresses and sensible shoes. For any formal occasion, she wore a hat covered with lots of little flowers. One of my grandfather's biographers said she was homely, but I don't think that was true. Surprisingly, she had her underwear custom made, and once gave me a lovely slip in pink satin with my monogram (J.K.W., the same as hers) written in blue lace at the top. My grandmother was an accomplished equestrienne in her youth and, riding sidesaddle, won many silver trophies. Some of them—monogrammed with her initials, J.K.W.—came into my possession as her namesake.

A different side of Grandmother comes out in a story written by Catherine Small, later Catherine Keesey, in the Wheaton College alumni notes about her first year there, in 1902:

> Wheaton never encouraged visits from beaux. Not many men had the courage to call on a girl there. One day, to my amazement, I received a note from Charlotte Keesey's older brother, Vincent. I hardly knew him and thought his mother had probably asked him to come see me. I asked permission to have him call and it was granted and the day set. The windows in Metcalf Hall were full of girls watching for Vincent, for we were not allowed to introduce a caller to anyone, but had to entertain him in a formal reception room. At last Vincent came and we were seated in stiff chairs facing each other and I was doing my best to be entertaining when suddenly there was a knock on the door. I said, "Come in," and who should appear but Jeannette with her hair pulled back tight in a knot and dressed as a maid with a white apron and said in the most awful Irish brogue, "You're wanted at the telephone, Mum." I tried not to look amazed and excused myself and left the room presumably to answer the telephone. When I got outside I found no one in sight so in a few minutes I returned. Not long afterwards there was another knock and when I said, "Come in," Nell appeared in a black dress with a dainty sheer white apron and cap, looking as pretty as could be, with a tray with tea and said, "Would you like some tea, Miss?" I thanked her and she put down the tray and I poured tea. I tried to act as if this was what happened when a man called on a girl at Wheaton. The

girls were determined to see Vincent and he and I laughed many times over his visit to Wheaton for I married him a few years later.

Granny was quite old-fashioned about what things were and weren't suitable for me. When I was fourteen, all the girls my age wore Tangee, a hideous lipstick with an orange tinge. One day, I wore it on a visit to my grandmother. This was the first time I had taken the train by myself to New York. A black man was seated across from me. Around half-way into the city he opened his fly, pulled out his penis, and began to masturbate. I was like a deer caught in the headlights and couldn't decide what to do. I felt it might be rude to move my seat, as he seemed to be working so hard and earnestly. I watched respectfully and was relieved when he finished, though I didn't exactly understand what had happened and never mentioned it to a soul. After meeting my train, my grandmother immediately called my father to tell him that lipstick was unsuitable for a fourteen-year-old girl. My father got furious with my mother, who in turn was not happy with me.

(My father was also horrified when, at fifteen, I started to wear eye makeup. One night before a date, I came into the library, where my father was interrogating my terrified cavalier. He saw me enter the room and said loudly, to my utter mortification, "What's that *black junk* on your eyes?")

On that same visit, I think, my grandmother took me to the movie *Marjorie Morningstar*, which captivated me—at least for a while. She thought it was too risqué and made us leave about halfway through, taking me instead to see *A Dog of Flanders*, which I didn't enjoy nearly as much. But she encouraged my reading, and we always went to the bookstore together to pick out a new title. When we returned to her apartment, she would read aloud to me, even when I was quite old.

My uncle Dick even built a small house for her on his property in New Canaan after my grandfather died, and during the summer, if my father had to come back from Maine to work at IBM, he used to stay with her.

My father told me that my grandfather's character was so strong that my grandmother's personality was overshadowed. But she was no pushover. As my father recounted in his autobiography, Grandfather put endless demands on her in the early days of IBM, and after ten years of strife she asked for a divorce. "I told him I couldn't stand it anymore"—words that were strikingly similar to the ones exchanged between my father and mother after his heart attack.

My grandfather and Queen Wilhelmina in 1942

"Tom," my grandmother told my father, "he looked so shocked, so upset, that I realized how deeply he loved me — and I never brought it up again." After she made the decision to preserve the marriage, she never complained again. If a crowd showed up and she had no one to help in the kitchen, she'd smile and say, "The cook is off today, but we have some sandwiches and fruit."

In 1938, my grandparents took a tour abroad, stopping in Albania, Greece, Romania, England, and France. It was all very grand. They hobnobbed with now-forgotten kings, queens, and lesser royalty, as well as assorted aristocrats and political leaders — the "highborn," as my father put it.

In Albania they were received by King Zog and his lovely young wife, Geraldine, and they dined on solid gold plates, with dinner and dancing until 3:00 a.m.. As they traveled, there were rumblings of war and much anxiety. My grandmother would later describe England's war preparations, including the evacuation of children. My grandparents traveled with a lady's maid, Ernestine, and my grandfather had a valet — all very *Downton Abbey*-ish!

In 1942 Queen Wilhelmina of the Netherlands paid a visit to the United States, and my grandfather was her escort and even gave a birthday party for the

Holiday reunion at Meadowcroft Lane. (I am the tallest girl; my brother, the second boy.)

future queen Juliana! That same year he wrote a book: *An overview of the historic visit of Queen Wilhelmina of the Netherlands to the Dominion of Canada and the United States of America.*

The entire Watson family—my grandparents, their four children, and their spouses, and eventually eighteen grandchildren—were together for all major holidays and frequently spent time at my grandparents' country house in New Canaan. The third generation sat at the children's table, and my cousin Mary Buckner and I, as the two oldest girls, were in charge of making sure the little ones behaved.

In the late '40s and '50s, when IBM had country clubs for its employees, the company had "family" parties for the IBM family. I remember going to one as a little girl with my grandfather and singing along to the IBM rally song:

There's a thrill in store for all,
For we're about to toast
The corporation known in every land.
We're here to cheer each pioneer

And also proudly boast
Of that "man of men," our friend and guiding hand.
The name of T. J. Watson means a courage none can stem;
And we feel honored to be here to toast the "IBM."

EVER ONWARD — EVER ONWARD!
That's the spirit that has brought us fame!
We're big, but bigger we will be.
We can't fail, for all can see
That to serve humanity has been our aim!
Our products now are known, in every zone,
Our reputation sparkles like a gem!
We've fought our way through — and new
Fields we're sure to conquer too
For the EVER ONWARD I.B.M.

EVER ONWARD — EVER ONWARD!
We're bound for the top to never fall!
Right here and now we thankfully
Pledge sincerest loyalty
To the corporation that's the best of all!
Our leaders we revere, and while we're here,
Let's show the world just what we think of them!
So let us sing, men! SING, MEN!
Once or twice then sing again
For the EVER ONWARD I.B.M.

Over the years, sons and daughters of IBM employees have mentioned to me how much the Country Clubs meant to them. One said to me, "I would never have learned to swim if it hadn't been for IBM."

When I look back at the paternalistic culture at IBM in those days, and compare it to the way big companies operate today — with their impersonal human-resources departments, obsession with profits and share price, and astronomical executive salaries — I can't help but think that corporate America has lost its heart.

At an IBM Christmas party. I am on Santa's lap.

Mummy, Grandfather, Daddy, Grandmother, and three girls. I am the tallest!

Business leaders were admired when my grandfather and father ran IBM. They were celebrated in newspapers and national magazines, not just because they brought prosperity to the country, but also because they had a personal connection with their employees and their customers.

With Grandfather: "I felt totally adored."

March 25th 1950.

My Precious Promise.
         I have just learned
that you have been to the
Hospital and I cannot understand
why a pin was put into four food,
I have never eaten pins, but
I do not believe I would like
them, when I return home I want
you to tell me all about it, but
please do not ask me to eat pins.
         Granny and I have a very nice
time here in Lima, we leave on
monday for Equidor Columbia and
Panama then New York.
         I think it would be very nice if
you would take me for a trip to
Atlantic City, soon after I return,
just you and I alone, think it
over and let me know.
                  I send you loads of
         love and seven kisses.
                           Grandfather

One of the lovely letters Grandfather wrote me—in this case, after I swallowed a pin.

Chapter Three

My father was a mythic figure, blessed by the gods in so many ways. He was charismatic, smart, funny, and devoted to his family. He was a seasoned pilot, a renowned sailor, Mr. Twinkle Toes on the dance floor, a skier, a diplomat, an occasional chef, and, of course, head of one of the largest companies in America. He was like a Shakespearean hero with a fatal flaw. The real tragedy was that he knew it and was unable to change. As he wrote in his 1990 autobiography, *Father, Son & Co.: My Life at IBM and Beyond*, co-authored with Peter Petre, "If my disposition had been easier, I might have had a brilliant career as a father, because I did a lot of imaginative things for my children."

Even today, twenty-five years after my father published his autobiography, and twenty-two years after his death, when I see his face smiling benignly out at me from the cover, I feel a stab of fear. Other emotions follow — love, respect, and gratitude — more in keeping with our public image. I have struggled to come to terms with my childhood, which was quite different from the way it appears in family photos, and with the haunting parallels between my father's childhood and my own. We experienced similar feelings of alienation, depression, and sibling rivalry, and he loved and feared his father just as I loved and feared him.

His temper got the better of him, leaving wounds that occasionally flare up even today. I still am extremely uncomfortable with conflict of any kind and loud voices. Until fairly recently, I remembered Christmas mainly as the time of year when my father became inconsolably depressed, triggering the same emotion in me. The memory of how my parents sparred at the dining room table still causes my stomach to clench.

When my father was thirteen, he "began to suffer recurring depressions so deep that no one knew where they were going to lead." He had to be urged to eat and bathe. He couldn't read a book. He would recover after about thirty days, but after six months he would fall into the abyss again. "I'd slip from...thinking I was going crazy, to a stage where I didn't know what was going on around me." He also had suicidal thoughts, telling his brother Arthur, known as Dick, that "if I die, be sure to tell Mother and Dad that it's not their fault."

In Greenwich, Daddy seemed to revert to the kind of depression that he experienced as a teenager. The blues came like clockwork at Christmas. He locked himself in his dressing room, which had a bed and TV, as well as clothes closets and a bath, and my mother would beg him to come out. This happened occasionally at other times of the year, too. "When I couldn't bend my wife and children to my will, I'd feel totally thwarted and boxed in," he wrote. "...The only thing I could do was hole up." Sometimes my mother would call his brother Dick in New Canaan, and he would drive down and "draw me back into my world."

The tense relationship between my father and grandfather continued until grandfather died, in 1956, when I was eleven. My father said that they'd get into "hellacious" fights nearly every month. "They were savage, primal, and unstoppable," he wrote. "When he criticized me, I found it impossible to hold back my rage."

I never remember my father sitting down and reading during the day. Daddy was a dervish of activity, always eager to try something new, the more dangerous the better. A psychiatrist would probably peg him as a manic-depressive who used frenetic activity to prolong his "up" periods and keep his demons at bay.

He learned to fly as a teenager and continued to do so all through college. At eighteen, with his old friend Bill Pattison, he flew to Dallas to a deb party and then on to St. Louis. Before their first sortie, neither had ever flown at night. One said to the other, "I think we just turn on the lights." They were the original young invincibles.

I began flying with him when I was small, and kept going aloft with him as his planes got larger and more sophisticated. He built a landing strip on our property in North Haven and often created quite a stir when coming in for a landing. We'd hear crackling on the radio, and then he would announce himself. "This is N6789er, N6789er. Do you copy Oak Hill? Susan, get your goddamn donkeys off the runway." Susan would hop on her motorcycle barefoot and round up her wayward pets.

He got his jet license at age sixty-five (the oldest person ever to do so), and then learned to fly a helicopter. Whenever my husband Alex and I arrived at our house in the family compound, my father would hover outside our barn in his helicopter and peek into our huge glass window, wearing big goggles, with his white hair blowing wildly in the wind, giving him a slightly demented look.

He took up ballooning his late sixties and began flying a stunt plane when he was seventy. He entertained his grandchildren by doing barrel rolls and other crazy stunts while releasing smoke from the back of the plane. The grandchildren were enthralled. But I was terrified that they might be forever traumatized if their daredevil grandfather crashed to the ground. My mother-in-law Edwina hated small planes. When she came to visit us in North Haven, my father thought it would be a great treat for her to accompany him in his helicopter while he pointed out the interesting sights. He happily zoomed down to show her various small islands, not realizing that the flight was sheer hell for Edwina. She didn't visit us in Maine again until after Daddy died.

As Daddy neared eighty, he had a few scary episodes while flying, and he was afraid the FAA might revoke his license. Usually Jimmy Brown, our Maine caretaker, helped him roll his stunt plane out of the hangar, but one day Daddy decided he would do it himself. He rolled the plane out and got in, not noticing that he hadn't closed the canopy all the way. As the plane was taking off, the canopy opened completely. Daddy tried to close it and crashed the plane. Jimmy heard the noise and came running. He saw Daddy emerge from the ruined plane and go into the house. When he came back out, he was as cool as someone who had taken a minor spill while roller skating.

"Well, I guess I did that right."

"What did you do?" asked Jimmy.

"I took a slug of bourbon, two tranquilizers, and ordered a new plane."

The next problem was dealing with the corpus delicti. Daddy didn't want the FAA to find out about the crash, so he and Jimmy flew over to the mainland in another plane and rented a truck, which they took back on the North Haven ferry. Jimmy dismantled the plane and they loaded it into the truck. My father hired someone to drive it to Vermont and deliver it to one of his flying buddies, who then got rid of the "evidence."

My father's second love was sailing. I began spending time on his yachts when I was a young girl. Daddy had different yachts over the years, each suited to his style of life at that time. They were all called *Palawan* after a beautiful island in the South Seas he visited at the end of the Second World War. The earlier boats were more geared toward racing, the middle ones were for adventure and travel, and the late ones were for comfortable family cruising. I can remember him building a mock-up of the main cabin of one of our *Palawan*s in his study in our Greenwich home. I loved sailing on the *Palawan* on lazy summer afternoons, with my father towing me behind on a raft and the cool salty water streaming over me. He became quite a renowned ocean sailor, winning the Bermuda Race several times, and he later traced Captain James Cook's voyages in the Pacific.

When I was a junior at boarding school, my father invited my roommate, Suzannah Hornburg, and her father to sail back with us after the Bermuda race. They both accepted, neither having had much experience sailing. I said to Suzannah in a superior tone, "You will probably get seasick, but I never do." We started off in beautiful weather. But by the second day the sky was looking ominous, and we wound up out of radio contact for several days, caught in a hurricane. My father reveled in the storm. He was the old man against the sea. He organized a sea anchor behind the boat to stabilize us and slow her down. All the men wore harnesses to attach themselves to a railing, because there was a real danger of being blown off the slippery decks. Suzannah and I, banished from the deck, stayed in a cabin below, scared witless. Everyone (myself included) got seasick. Here is my father's description of the storm:

> We had cleared St. George's Channel in the morning and by nightfall were about 60 miles off the islands, when Bermuda Harbor radio began forecasting strong winds in our area. We battened things down for a rough night, and the wind, blowing about Force Six by midnight, had increased to a full gale by dawn. By noon it was gusting to well over 70 knots.
>
> The crew was below except for our professional, my son Tom, and myself, and we had our hands full. We had moved progressively down to a reefed mainsail, storm jib, no mainsail, then no sail at all, and finally we began to prepare for a full hurricane. We had oil ready in one of the heads to pump overboard if necessary to calm the seas, and running

before the gale with bare poles, we trailed astern two long loops of rope, which were secured on opposite sides of our taffrail. These helped greatly to slow the boat and quiet the seas, so that the cockpit filled less frequently. But to carry the ropes from the foredeck, where they were stored, to the stern was a major task. I found I couldn't stand against the wind, but had to crawl forward slowly, snapping and re-snapping my safety harness as I went. The roar of the wind was monstrous and the only way to communicate with anyone else on deck was by hand signal.

My father made his most ambitious sail in 1974, when he was sixty. Three years earlier, in Greenwich Hospital, recovering from a heart attack that prompted his retirement from IBM, he began dreaming about sailing up the coast of Greenland to Etah, the abandoned Eskimo settlement where Admiral Robert Peary started the final leg of his voyage of discovery to the North Pole. Wanting a boat for voyaging, rather than speed, Daddy summoned Olin Stephens, the yacht designer, and Paul Wolter, the professional captain of the second *Palawan*, a fifty-eight-foot yawl. The three of them sketched out plans for a successor *Palawan*, a sixty-eight-foot ketch. It was built at a boatyard in Bremen, Germany, and in 1973 Daddy sailed it home across the Atlantic so he could learn its quirks.

The voyage to Greenland was not for the faint of heart. My father and his crew of seven threaded their way between submerged "blue band ice" and giant cakes of white ice on the surface. A telegram interrupted the voyage: YOU MUST COME HOME. His brother Dick had died, and Daddy flew back for the funeral. He left my mother in Connecticut to console my aunt Nancy, and he returned at once to the *Palawan*. "I was in no state to be of use to anyone," he said. The *Palawan* managed to get far north of where any pleasure boat had gone, but was stymied by thickening ice. Daddy and his crew were only 150 miles from Etah and 770 miles from the Pole.

My father was crazy about motorcycles and rode them throughout his life. He also had motorcycles for his children to ride on, and Olive and Lucinda were great enthusiasts. He often rode his motorcycle to work at IBM, dressed head to toe in black leather. Then Superman would go into his office and emerge like Clark Kent in a conservative pin-striped suit.

In 1967, when he was fifty-three, he went to Zermatt and had an exhilarating time skiing the lower heights of the Matterhorn. True to form, he became obsessed

Daddy at the summit of the Matterhorn

with climbing the Matterhorn, one of the highest mountains (14,692 feet) in the Alps, straddling Italy and Switzerland. This was another of his "dream" adventures that he fulfilled after leaving IBM. Recently my sister-in-law told me the story of Daddy's climb. Evidently, his guide Paul Julen said "I can get you up, but I can't get you down." Daddy insisted, and so they started at 10:30 at night, and after climbing all night, arrived at the top at mid-morning the next day. A helicopter was flying overhead, and Paul said, "Lie down." Daddy lay down, indicating he couldn't climb down, and eventually had an exciting transfer by rope to the helicopter, which couldn't land on the peak. When Daddy got back to the base of the mountain, he called President Jimmy Carter and said: "I just climbed the Matterhorn, so I guess I can be ambassador to Russia." He was appointed in the summer of 1979, in the third year of Carter's one term in office.

Typical of a man of action, my father sometimes got out ahead of himself. Two of my younger sisters spent a summer in Lapland, Finland, participating in an international program and staying with a family there. While visiting my sisters, my father impulsively invited two of the family's daughters to visit us in New York. This turned out to have been a somewhat misguided decision, as neither of my sisters especially liked the "Little Laps," as we called them. Daddy flew them to New York and immediately took them with the family to dinner at Lutèce on

My father on his unicycle (photo by Toni Frissell)

East Fiftieth Street, at the time a very fancy and expensive French restaurant that was one of his favorites. The Little Laps dozed through every course, and later fell sound asleep at the Broadway production of *Fiddler on the Roof*. Everyone, including the Little Laps, breathed a sigh of relief when the visit ended.

Daddy liked nothing better than scooping up a group of kids and taking them on an adventure—on his boat, out camping, or simply in one of his old cars to get ice cream cones. When I was in ninth grade, he invited me and a group of my friends for a cruise on his boat. This made me briefly popular with my Greenwich Country Day classmates who came along, but two weeks afterward I felt as isolated as ever.

When I was sixteen, we rented a house in Camden, Maine, where my father had spent summers growing up. One lovely summer day, my father, Helen, and I sailed to a nearby island and cooked hamburgers for lunch. Just as we were finishing we heard a voice. My father leapt up, his face white, and started searching the uninhabited island. After we'd made sure that no one was there, we got on the boat and headed for home. Daddy turned to me and said, "Jen, did you hear a voice?" I replied that I had but hadn't been able to hear what it was saying. My father told me the voice had said, "Are you all right, Tommy?" He then said the only person who'd ever called him Tommy was his father, who had died years before. Daddy remarked that he was going through a hard time at IBM that summer. When we arrived home we told my mother about the voice, but she didn't take the account seriously. My father went on to deny it had happened, but years later he admitted it *had*. I thought about the voice: analyzed it with my friends and ultimately decided it was some beneficent being (my grandfather?) interested in my father's welfare.

My father used to buy all sorts of cheeses and delighted in tasting them. He enjoyed some classical music and would listen to Tchaikovsky over and over. He loved the ballet, and while I was at college I was thrilled when he gave me two tickets to see Margot Fonteyn and Rudolf Nureyev in *Romeo and Juliet*. Years later, when he was the ambassador to the Soviet Union, he went to the ballet as often as possible. My mother told me that, before attending a performance, he would listen to the music and dance some of the steps in his dressing room.

He and my mother also enjoyed ballroom dancing, and my father wanted his daughters to be good dancers. Occasionally he would take my mother and some of his older daughters to the Maisonette in the St. Regis Hotel on East Fifty-Fifth Street, where he'd dance with each of us in turn.

My father admired my love of books, and sometimes he'd ask me to recount the plots of novels I was reading. I remember in particular giving him a summary of *Crime and Punishment* when I was in my teens. I told him how Raskolnikov felt he had the right to kill a pawnbroker because he could use her money to greater good. Daddy was fascinated by this moral inversion and cited it in some of his speeches. Later, when I was running Books & Co. on Madison Avenue, he kept asking for a definitive list of the hundred great books, so that he could start reading them.

He was also passionate about poetry. He grew up at a time when it was a much greater part of the school curriculum than it is now, and when memorization was an important part of study. He liked Kipling, and "When Earth's Last Picture Is Painted" was one of his favorites. At age twenty, he memorized a parody of Robert W. Service by Edward E. Paramore Jr., "The Ballad of Yukon Jake."

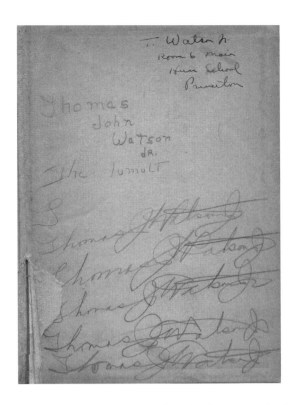

Daddy practices his signature in his schoolboy poetry book

OH THE NORTH COUNTREE is a hard countree
That mothers a bloody brood;
And its icy arms hold hidden charms
For the greedy, the sinful and lewd.
And strong men rust, from the gold and the lust
That sears the Northland soul,
But the wickedest born, from the Pole to the Horn,
Is the Hermit of Shark Tooth Shoal.

Oh how I loved the word "lewd." When I pronounced it slowly, it sounded almost pornographic. I have my father's old poetry text from high school, and it is touching to see how he practiced his signature on the endpapers of the book.

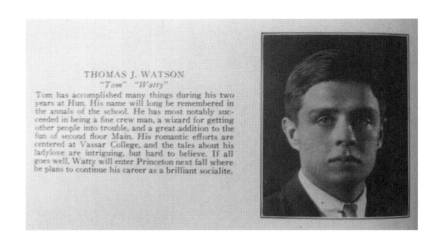

THOMAS J. WATSON
"Tom" "Watty"

Tom has accomplished many things during his two
years at Hun. His name will long be remembered in
the annals of the school. He has most notably suc-
ceeded in being a fine crew man, a wizard for getting
other people into trouble, and a great addition to the
fun of second floor Main. His romantic efforts are
centered at Vassar College, and the tales about his
ladylove are intriguing, but hard to believe. If all
goes well, Watty will enter Princeton next fall where
he plans to continue his career as a brilliant socialite.

After six years in high school, Daddy's blurb in the Hun School yearbook

My father's late interest in literature was his way of making up for what he had missed at school. To say that he was no scholar is an understatement. He stayed back two grades in high school, and when he finally graduated from the Hun School in New Jersey, he had been rejected by Princeton and everywhere else. "Tommy, get in the car," my grandfather said. "We're going to drive around the country until we find a college that will accept you."

Good fortune struck when they visited the admissions office at Brown University. This is how my father described the way my grandfather introduced himself: "I'm Tom Watson, I run the IBM company, and my son would like to consider coming to Brown. By the way, who is the president of Brown?'"

"The admissions guy said, 'Clarence Barbour.'"

"'That's very interesting,' said Dad. "'He was my pastor when I lived in Rochester, New York.'"

"We went to Clarence Barbour's office, said hello, and Barbour got some-body to show us around campus. When we returned, the admissions officer was looking at my record. He said, 'He's not very good but we'll take him.'"

Daddy lived up to his low expectations. He failed American history twice, provoking the professor to say, "I would like to welcome all the new class mem-bers — and hello again, Mr. Watson."

The wheels had been greased for my father, and not for the last time. When he joined IBM, he was the fair-haired boy, because he was the boss's son. By throwing business his way, and advancing his career, his supervisors hoped to advance their own. He spent his whole life trying to get out of his father's shadow and prove himself a success in his own right. I can see, in retrospect, how much pressure he put on himself, and how much of it he brought home with him. When his safety valve blew, and he lost his temper, everyone in the family paid the price.

My father loved to sing and tell jokes, and he had a gift for accents. A lot of his stories would be offensive today, but in the '50s ethnic humor scarcely raised an eyebrow — except if you were the butt of the joke. Once he told one of my younger sisters a rhyme that began:

> Ching ching chinamen sitting on a fence
> trying to make a dollar off of fifteen cents

When she told this to her second-grade class, her teacher, Ms. Chang, was not amused.

When Daddy was relaxed and happy, no one was more fun. But he could erupt at any time. You could be talking to him as if he were the easiest person in the world, laughing and having a great conversation, and then something would set him off, and he'd become a totally different and scary person. "WHAT DO YOU MEAN BY THAT!" he would demand in a threatening voice through gritted teeth. Then I would frantically backpedal and try to smooth things out, but by then the damage had been done.

Daddy believed in quite a regimented schedule for us. Even on weekends we had to be up, dressed and down to breakfast at 7:30 — no sleeping in! (Today on weekends I still get a kick out of lounging around in my bathrobe!) We usually had some family activity, such as a bike ride, or sailing on my father's boat. During the summer not much spontaneity was involved, as we had to announce at breakfast what we were doing for lunch or dinner, and once "the help" had been alerted, there was no going back!

We had quite an early curfew, and when we were invited to parties, my father made me call to make sure an adult would be there... Also: Absolutely no TV during the day, and only two hours a night on weekends. Turn off all lights before you leave your room. I can remember that, one night, when we were out, my father, removed from our rooms all the lightbulbs that had been left on, and then, when we returned, chuckled in his room while we complained that something was wrong with the lights. When we were at our ski house in Vermont, we had to be on the lifts when the slopes opened, and we couldn't come home until they closed.

Greenwich was very bland and waspy in the '50s, and my father felt his daughters should have husbands that would fit in. Once, when I was around seventeen, I was going up in a chairlift with him, and my father asked me, "So, Jen—would you ever go out with a Jew?" (He pronounced it *tcheww*.) "Oh yes, Daddy," I answered eagerly, even though I didn't know any Jews. "Would you marry one?" he went on, his voice becoming edgy. "Oh yes, Daddy," I said, pleased to see that I was getting a rise out of him. We went through the same scenario for blacks (except he called them Negroes), with increasing agitation on my father's part. After I married, I was delighted to learn that my husband Alex—although not raised Jewish—was the great-grandson of Orthodox Jews.

Even though my father was not big on intermixing within his own family, he was very much for equal opportunity at IBM. He even told some officials in a Southern town that he would put an IBM plant there on the condition that the company could hire an equal number of whites and blacks. At the request of Robert Kennedy, he put an IBM plant in a particularly poor area of Bedford Stuyvesant, Brooklyn. My son, Ralph, recently sent me an article citing this IBM plant as a model for how a corporation could help an inner-city community and still make a profit. At IBM my father put in place a policy barring racial discrimination, becoming one of the first CEOs of a large company to do so.

Like my grandfather, he was a staunch Democrat, which used to surprise people. Unlike a lot of wealthy people today, he believed in paying his fair share of taxes and providing services for people less fortunate than he.

As a company, IBM has maintained an ethos of social responsibility. All of Thomas Watson Sr.'s grandchildren were recently invited to the company's hundredth anniversary. Watching a film about the history of IBM, I felt very proud of my father and grandfather.

I also posed with the famous IBM Watson computer, named after my grandfather, which showed that artificial intelligence was not as far off as most people thought. Initially developed to answer questions on the quiz show *Jeopardy*, it stored 200 million pages of information, including all of Wikipedia, and responded to questions posed in English. IBM Watson got a lot of publicity when it thumped two former *Jeopardy* champions. Beginning in 2013, the machine has been put to use in a variety of data-intensive fields, beginning with evaluating options for treating lung cancer at Memorial Sloan-Kettering Cancer Center in New York.

When I was about twelve I came home from Greenwich Country Day one afternoon and told my father that the other kids were teasing me about being rich.

"Are we rich, Daddy?" I asked.

"No, we're not rich. We have *some* money," was his reply.

Daddy was funny about money. Even though he owned, at one point, four houses, two apartments, a Learjet, a helicopter, a yacht, and a big collection of old cars, he felt he lived a modest life and didn't want to discuss money with his children. He was concerned about saving money and delighted in driving in and out of the city using the Willis Avenue Bridge and avoiding the toll. Daddy suggested to my mother that she could save money by buying day-old bread at the nearby Wonder Bread factory.

Daddy was quite controlling and wanted to reach beyond the grave to determine the future of my parents' lovely house in Maine. The house was built in two sections linked by an arched breezeway. He was afraid the six children might fight over it, so he left instructions that it should be blown up.

I remember telling this to Fran Lebowitz, who responded in great indignation, "How can your father blow up a house? I need a house!"

My mother responded by blowing up half the house. I could imagine my parents' discussion in the afterlife—my mother, with wide eyes hands raised to her mouth, saying: "Oh, Tom! You meant the WHOLE house?"

When I launched Books & Co. in my early thirties, half of the start-up funds were lent to me by my father. I was advised to make it a corporation and told my father smugly that this was great, because it meant that if the bookstore went bankrupt, we wouldn't have to pay anyone back. He was horrified by my cavalier attitude. "If the bookstore fails," he said sternly, "you and I will pay back every single publisher and vendor that is owed money." After I thought about it, I realized he was right, and when Books & Co. closed, twenty years later, I repaid everyone.

When I was young and went on trips with the family, I knew I was traveling with an unusually handsome and charismatic companion—think, an early version of Jon Hamm. I could hear people whisper, "There's Tom Watson of IBM."

The eye-catching IBM man in an official corporate picture

Aside from being handsome, he had the kind of magnetism that attracted every eye in the room. If my mother was an "it" girl, my father was an "it" guy. Often my dates would come to see me and end up falling in love with my father, or else my mother — though husband-to-be Alex mercifully didn't develop a crush on either one, just one on me.

When we travelled, my parents would frequently be invited out for dinner by the American ambassador or a country's political leaders or royalty. My father seemed to know everyone and had friends in every big city, not a few of whom were on the board of IBM. Some of the board members were presidents of major companies all over the world. Our family was featured in *Sports Illustrated* and *Life,* and Daddy appeared alone in countless others.

~

In 1957, my parents built our ski house in Stowe. With the help of a local architect, my father and mother designed the house so that it had two dormitories: one where all the girls slept and the other for my lucky brother, who could fill the space with his friends. The house opens up into a cathedral-like space with various "conversation pits" (which were big at the time). An open counter marks off the

CLOSE-UP

**Busy days
for IBM's
Tom Watson**

MIDGET CAR, a Messerschmitt, is used
at home. Daughters are Susan, 5 (*front*),
Cindy, 8, Olive, 9, and Jeannette, 11.

CYCLING with his wife Olive and Susan,
Mr. Watson rides in Greenwich.
He married his wife, a model, in 1941.

*"My brother and I both have little
foreign cars. The whole neighborhood
watches us when we race
each other backwards. It's very much
like an airplane with a bucket seat."*

*"We concentrate on the sports we can
all do together. Bicycling is a wonderful
conditioner for the skiing we do in
winter. My wife is the person
who really makes the family click."*

TOP: My father teaches my brother how to shoot in *Life*
BOTTOM: *Life* profiles the Watson family

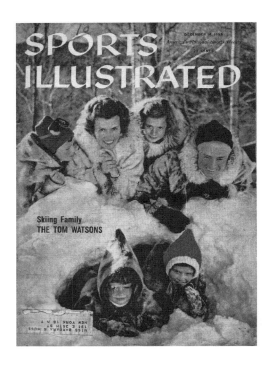

I'm on the top of the heap on *Sports Illustrated*'s cover

kitchen, making it easy to cook and serve. The house, now owned by my brother and my niece, is like a '50s museum, with Eames plastic chairs (now quite valuable) in front of the kitchen counter, and other period pieces. We loved it as kids, and still do.

Downstairs in the basement was a play area for the children, with a ping-pong table and a seating area with a few board games. One year when we were teenagers we had a New Year's Eve party down there, and my father later heard that the lights had been switched off around midnight. After that, he had an electrician rig up a light in his bedroom that would go *on* as soon as the lights in the basement went *off*. There would be no hanky-panky going on under his roof.

There are still signs in my father's handwriting posted around the house, as though he is speaking to us from beyond the grave:

> Turn off the lights when you are out of the room.
> – *The Management*

My parents were both good skiers and made sure we all had private instruction so that we could be good as well. The family went on skiing trips to Vail, Zermatt, and Squaw Valley. One sunny day in Vail, my sisters and I were lathering our faces with sunscreen in different strengths, and just as I'd announced I was using a lotion with a SPF of 50, my mother swept over and said emphatically, "Don't talk about the numbers—your father doesn't <u>believe</u> in them!"

My father could be quite ingenious when it came to punishments. I remember my little sisters, after committing some offense, were made to drag their donkeys around the property in North Haven. When one of my sisters, a four-year-old at that time, was whining while we were out on our lobster boat, he left her on a bell buoy and didn't come back for ten minutes. My mother would send me to my room as punishment—which in fact was a treat, since I could do what I did best: lollygag about and read.

I read so much that my father called me *Madame Nose in Book*. Once, in total frustration at my obsessive reading, he said threateningly, "I am going to build you a little castle in France where you can read all day." I thought this would be wonderful and imagined myself as the "Little Lame Prince," reading as much as I wanted and flying around on my magic carpet to view my kingdom.

Away from work, my father was always in motion—flying, ballooning, riding motorcycles (or his unicycle), tooling around in old cars. He crammed all sorts of activities into our trips abroad. He was also a natural leader. If he had been an infantry officer, men would have followed him over the top, whatever the risks. Brendan Gill, a friend of mine, described this quality in a passage quoted in Lynne Tillman's *Bookstore*, which recounted my days running Books & Co.:

> He was one of the most extraordinary people I ever met, truly charismatic—a cheesy word now, charismatic, but he was, to the point where if he told you that something was so, it was not only so, but you would back it with your own life. For example, once he invited me to fly up to Stowe for a skiing weekend, and we were to meet in Westchester. A blizzard came, and the airport was closed. "I'm going out, do you want to come, Brendan?" I said, "Of course I'll come." Because it was Tom Watson. It was a plane he had not flown often before, and he was going to fly himself—he had a copilot, but he had a book of instructions spread on his legs, and then he said into the microphone, "I'm taking

responsibility for this flight, and I'm getting out of here." They put the lights on and we went off in the snow. When we got up in the air, it turned out that the airport in Stowe was also closed, and Tom had gotten in touch with somebody and they opened up another airport somewhere else, and we came down at another airport, newly plowed, just for us, and Tom. This was the commonplace."

At my father's funeral, Vartan Gregorian succinctly captured the virtues and flaws of his friend:

> Tom Watson was an extraordinary man, a complex man. He was both an actor and an observer. He was an independent man, a man of humor. Who else, after all, would take the president of Brown in a helicopter and right before takeoff say, "I've only had two heart attacks so don't worry."
>
> He was a man of laughter. He was a man of anger. He was an energetic man, demanding, impatient, hot-tempered, difficult, kind, generous, and a wonderful man. Tom was an idealist yet steeped in reality, a visionary who was master of all the details to make his vision a reality. He was an unyielding and relentless competitor, a pragmatist who disliked ideological dogmatists and exhibitionists on the left as well as on the right of the political spectrum. He was devoted to his friends and valued integrity, loyalty, and competence. A man of privilege, he considered service to one's community, one's nation, one's country a social and moral obligation.

Before my father died, when he was very ill and in the hospital, he put a large sign on the door: "No Religious People Allowed." This was the last sign from a man who liked to put up signs everywhere. My family and I had been vacationing in Florida, and I called when we returned on New Year's Eve to ask my mother whether I should come out that night to visit, but she discouraged me, and the next morning he was dead. Quite a New Year's resolution! I don't think he had enjoyed his life after his stroke six months earlier, as he had no longer been able to ride a motorcycle or fly his plane by himself. His last meal was a McDonald's Big Mac, which he asked my mother to pick up on her way to the hospital.

Chapter Four

Everyone remarked on my mother's beauty—friends, relatives, even shopkeepers. She had very dark brown hair, large brown eyes, and a slender figure; her chiseled bone structure and cheekbones held it all together. She was proud of her twenty-five-inch waist and exercised and dieted to maintain it. The moment she noticed a few extra pounds, she immediately cut back and ate cottage cheese and melon.

Her skin was quite dark and she never wrinkled, even though she sat in the sun whenever she could. She liked to walk barefoot as soon as the weather got warm. She was a great swimmer and taught me how to breathe in the water by putting my face in her sink and telling me to blow bubbles.

In the '50s everyone was quite formal. I don't remember my mother ever wearing pants, only dresses, skirts and sweaters, or suits. I recall one dress in particular: strapless, boned and short, in beige satin with a dark brown lace overlay. She looked so glamorous in it. I loved to watch her dress up for parties. She sat at the altar of her makeup table, applying rouge from a little round box from France, along with powder, bright red lipstick, mascara, and finally perfume—something delicious like Joy or Bellodgia. Women all smelled wonderful then, with distinctive, strong fragrances. Today, it seems, no one wears such feminine perfumes, favoring more unisex, organic scents.

My parents' friends also seemed to look like movie stars. The women were slender, well-groomed and coiffed, mainly blonde, dressed in lovely clothes. The men were distinguished and sophisticated, and equally well dressed. They always seemed to be having a wonderful time. It was the *Mad Men* '60s, and they drank and flirted a lot. The air buzzed with sexual electricity, and you didn't have to listen hard for rumors of extramarital affairs.

I was fascinated by my mother, but in a detached sort of way. It was as if Vivien Leigh were living in our house, and I had a studio pass to go into her dressing room. I longed for a mother like Marmee in *Little Women*, that I could curl up next to and pour out my troubles. I think my mother enjoyed spending weeks in the hospital after each baby was born; there, instead of playing a supporting role to my father, she was the center of attention—the star—and she was surrounded by flowers, champagne, and well-wishers.

My mother loved to give parties, a trait I inherited. From my parents' bedroom, I watched their guests dance along our terrace, the romantic music from the band floating up to me. I imagined being older, with a strapless boned dress of my own and an ardent, handsome boyfriend. My parents also threw festive costume parties. My son Matt recently gave me a book called *Bals: Legendary Costume Balls of the 20th Century* by the English writer Nicholas Foulkes. In the introduction, Hélène David-Weill wrote that people worked less and had more leisure time in previous decades. This was certainly true of my parents and their friends. They kept a better balance between work and play, and were blissfully unencumbered by political correctness.

Being popular with men was extremely important to my mother. When I was around nine, I mentioned that I thought one of her friends was especially pretty. "Yes," she said complacently, "but I am much more popular." Given my weight issues and other drawbacks, I could never make the same claim. After sixth grade, I went to sailing class, and at the end of the summer two boys invited me to the Yacht Club dance. My mother was so excited by my social success that she drove me to Manhattan to have lunch and shop for a special dress at Saks Fifth Avenue.

Before one dinner party, my mother went to Woolworth and bought fabric, ribbons, scissors, and straight pins, which she divided into eight packages. At the end of the dinner, each man was presented with one set and told to go off and design a dress for his dinner partner, with a time limit of half an hour. Couples disappeared all over the downstairs of our house. At one point the butler came to my mother and said, in an outraged tone (heavily accented), "Meesus Watson, Meesus X is een the kitchen in her slip with Meestair Y." There are pictures from the party—a few women kept their dresses on, allowing their dinner partner's creations to be designed over their clothes, but most were in slips (though not, thankfully, my mother), and some of the men took their designing duties very seriously. Of course, in the '50s women wore girdles, bras, and full slips, so they were quite covered up. Since women no longer wear slips, or often any underwear, it would be an awfully risqué party today. But even back then, it seemed quite erotic, with men and women going off to various parts of our house and the women removing their dresses. I think I would be horrified to go to a party like that now. However forty-five years ago I might have thought it was great.

My mother was rarely in a blue mood. She had joie de vivre and the ability to stay in the present and not linger on sad times. In part this was because she was not introspective and tended to focus on material things. Toward the end of her life, I remember her saying, "I'm the luckiest girl in the world. Who would have thought that little Olive Cawley from Montclair, New Jersey, would have had the life I've had? I've met everyone and gone to the most amazing parties."

Of course, in many ways she was destined for an extraordinary life. From the time she was fourteen she was a beauty. Every generation has "it" girls. These girls had an ineffable combination of looks, charm, and wit. They had dazzle, and they knew how to make an entrance. My mother was one of those girls.

One day, when I was about twelve, my mother had me stay home from school. Evidently Granny Watson had decided that her family's genealogy should be done and had hired a professional to do this. When the genealogist called to say he had discovered interesting things about the family and that he wanted to meet to discuss his findings, Mummy was terrified. I was delighted to have a respite from school, which I hated.

In the library, the genealogist told Mummy that the Field side of her family could be traced back to Colonial times, and they were quite respectable people. The Cawleys, to Mummy's surprise, were far more impressive. They were related to French kings and could be traced back to Charlemagne and even earlier. The irony was that the Watson line was quite undistinguished. Mummy was relieved but never seemed to take it that seriously. In 2010, two years after her death, I decided I wanted to learn more about my mother's background so I could understand her better. I knew virtually nothing about her family, her childhood, or her upbringing.

I called my mother's cousin Herman Froeb, and he shared many stories with me about my mother and grandmother.

Mummy was the granddaughter of Cornelius James Field of Chicago, an inventor who worked with Thomas Edison. Together they developed the storage batteries used in streetcars. After his success with Edison, he bought a sugar cane plantation in Cuba, where he took his wife and four daughters. But he died prematurely of typhoid, and his wife Agnes was left penniless at age fifty with four grown daughters. Through a kind doctor's lie, they received medical life insurance in the amount of $40,000, which, at the time, was enough to live on quite comfortably. They even spent summers on Shelter Island.

Even so, the girls were under pressure to find breadwinner husbands. Ethelwynne married Samuel Cawley Jr. a charming and handsome man, but sadly an alcoholic. Mummy once described her father standing at the top of the stairs drinking a martini: He stumbled and fell all the way down, but his martini glass stayed miraculously upright—a scene right out of a William Powell movie. They had two children: my mother, Olive, and her brother, Brice.

Her parents divorced when Mummy was about three. She was evidently traumatized by the split and stopped eating. Ethelwynne could not understand why Mummy wasn't eating and took her from doctor to doctor. Finally one asked if there had been a recent change in young Olive's life. When he heard of the divorce and that the little girl had been cut off from her father, he instituted weekly visitation rights, and young Olive started eating again.

Grandfather Cawley died penniless and an alcoholic. At one point, I heard, he came to our house begging for money. Rumor was that he became a bellhop in the Catskills. I never met him. My mother said Cawley's mother, who came from a well-off family, was charming and fun. But because she and her husband kept loaning money to their son, she too died almost penniless.

Mummy was always somewhat embarrassed by her mother, who like her father, had a weakness for alcohol. Mummy told me she used to come home from school to find her mother lying on her bed in a darkened room strewn with empty bottles. I remember Granny Bloodgood coming to stay with us when Daddy was away. Lucinda and I would dance on the lawn while she looked on, always with a drink in her hand.

Every summer, Mummy would go to stay in Long Island with her aunt, Edith Froeb, and her cousins Neal and Herman. Whenever Mummy spoke of these times, there was a lilt in her voice. She always slept with her grandmother, Agnes

LEFT: My great-grandparents, Agnes and Cornelius

RIGHT: Cornelius Field with his onetime partner, Thomas Edison

Field, whom she adored. In Long Island, Mummy learned to sail, racing with her cousin Neal and the garbage man as crew.

Herman remembers the many beaus who pursued Mummy. Jack Kennedy was one of her more illustrious suitors; they dated during his junior and senior years at Choate. According to Herman, Edith and her husband didn't much like young Kennedy when he visited their Westhampton house. They thought he was a "wise gazebo" (whatever that is). Also, he didn't dress properly enough (according to their standards) to be taking Olive out.

My mother was crazy about Jack Kennedy and was a fairly serious girlfriend of his, often attending Choate proms as his date. Every time a new biography of him came out, she asked me to look her up in the index, to see what was said about her. I recently googled my mother and this is what appeared:

"Olive Cawley was one of Jack's girlfriend [sic] during the spring of his last year at Choate. By the time he graduated from prep school she had become

My mother with Jack Kennedy

a regular date. He met her at the Choate spring dance and she was said to be very pretty.

"Ever the non-romantic, however, JFK had warned her: 'Don't fall in love with me!' In addition, Kennedy apparently regularly reported to Lem Billings on his ultimately unsuccessful attempts to have sexual intercourse with Olive."

I was touched to see he had saved a letter she wrote him after his book *Profiles in Courage* was published. She described staying with the family and how Joe Kennedy insisted everybody talk about important topics, usually political. My parents decided this would be good for us, and we took turns deciding the topic and then doing research on it. If you hadn't done research, you couldn't talk. This practice didn't last long, as most of us didn't do any research.

Another of Mummy's suitors in her late teens was Howard Hughes. Herman recalls him landing his seaplane on the beach near the Westhampton house, immaculately dressed in white ducks, a blue blazer, and a captain's hat. He was evidently a huge fan of Agnes Field, and he'd sometimes visit her and talk about events of the day, even when he wasn't going out with Mummy. Herman says Agnes cut a regal figure. She wore robes, and her hair was frequently pinned up with tortoise-shell combs. Mummy would always laugh while telling a story about her cousin Neal kissing a girl on the porch. Grandmother Field's bedroom was directly above, and to show her disapproval, she poured a bucket of water on their heads.

Mummy always insisted her parents were middle class. They had a maid, and her stepfather, Jack Bloodgood, worked for a bank. Even so, Mummy attended her school on an athletic scholarship and was captain of the hockey and basketball teams. She also said that part of the money she earned modeling helped to pay for her brother's braces.

Recalling a Choate prom, my mother told me a story that was amazing but nonetheless indicative of her determination. She felt her dress was a bit dowdy, and spied, in the ladies' room, a girl wearing the Perfect Dress. My mother asked if she could try it on, and as soon as she had, she raced out of the ladies' room and found her date. She spent the rest of the evening avoiding the other girl, who was wearing my mother's dowdy dress and desperately trying to get her own pretty dress back.

When my mother graduated from high school, she became a model with the prestigious Powers Agency, and her photographs appeared in all the leading women's magazines—including *Vogue* and *Harper's Bazaar*. She was selected as one of the ten most beautiful and most photographed girls in the country, and, along with the other anointed ones, she was flown to Hollywood to be in Walter Wanger's production *Vogues of 1938*.

Here is an excerpt about the girls from Joshua Logan's memoir, *Movie Stars, Real People, and Me* called "Bogey and the Petals":

Bogey shone when surrounded by girls. Men liked him, but women had him for breakfast.

I found that out while I was in Hollywood in 1936 working with Walter Wanger in *History Is Made at Night*. Bogey was shooting *Dead End* for Samuel Goldwyn on the same lot, and often came over between takes. Wanger, an aging Dartmouth smoothie, was all excited because he was about to start shooting *Vogues of 1938*, with the eight most beautiful models in the world.

I could tell he was in an amorous haze when I saw him staring at a slip of paper as though he were reading a pornographic novel. He

My mother as one of the ten most beautiful girls in America.
(She is the middle girl in the top two photos.)

handed me the slip. It read, "Tomorrow morning at ten o'clock we are testing Miss Aldredge, Miss Cawley, Miss C, Miss D, Miss E."

I said, "I sure would like to meet those girls."

Wanger jumped up suddenly with a startling thought. "You've got the setup"—I was sharing a house with Jimmy Stewart, Hank Fonda, and John Swope—"you'll give them a party. All of you at the house. I don't want any of these Hollywood press agents to make the girls feel commercial. This affair has to have class. I'll send over the food and drink, but you've got to distill the guest list. No other girls. Fuck them. At least two men for every girl, and they must be (1) single, (2) tall, dark, and handsome; and (3) gentlemen in evening dress—and, if possible, famous. Above all, eligible. Now call me if Jimmy, Hank, and Johnny Swope agree."

I called him and accepted his conditions, because my roommates fell over themselves approving. When I tried out the idea on several friends I again found roaring acceptance. One friend even offered to pretend to break up with his girlfriend until the party was over, but we wouldn't allow that.

I spent so many hours on the telephone extolling the exquisite perfection of these girls that I began to fantasize them as creatures descending on a light-blue-rosy cloud from the land of Venus half-way up the rainbow.

We signed up dashing Alan Marshall and bulky but affable Dick Foran and a few others, but I was aiming for the big-time Bogart. At first, he wasn't sure, but then I began my poem on the juicy wonders of these New York vestal virgins—the tactile loveliness, the curvilinear fleshiness of them—and before I knew it, Bogart had caught the fever. Although there was a very low-key, underlying hint of sex to the whole thing, the filthy word was never so much mentioned. Deep down, though, I was a little bit afraid that I oversold Bogart because I had a feeling that he was expecting to walk right into a Boticelli gang bang.

The anticipated day arrived and still none of us had laid an eye on any of the girls, although we had heard raves from the people in the studio who had met them or worked on their photographic tests.

Eight of us were assigned to pick up one girl apiece at eight o'clock Saturday night. We dressed in our white tie and tails and took off for the various addresses. John Swope picked up Katherine Aldredge and I picked up Olive Cawley. Olive was dark, perfectly featured and with a glowing ivory skin and black, twinkling eyes. Katherine Aldredge was taller, blonder, full of vivacity, and almost perfectly formed. The other six were either their equal or slightly more perfect.

We arrived at the house and I began serving drinks, but none of the girls took a drink. All they wanted was lemonade. This, of course, made the anxious men take slightly larger whiskeys.

When the girls in their pastel dresses were scattered about the living room, they were like beautiful petals fallen from a perfect magnolia blossom—unstained, unscarred, with pulpy fragrance. And the language in the room became a little more circumspect. "Damns" and "hells" were increasingly difficult to find and certainly never "goddamns" or "Jesus Christs." I was beginning to be afraid that there was going to be a sudden avalanche, that the men were just going to storm out of the place, yelling bloody murder that they had been hoodwinked.

But not at all. Instead, they soon stopped drinking, too, and after dinner, for want of music to dance by, we began playing games—charades and musical chairs. Jimmy did a few card tricks. It was perhaps the most innocent evening any of us had spent since we were adolescents.

When the party was over and we had driven the magnolia petals home, we came back into the room and found that everyone had gone but Bogey, who was sitting there in an inkily thoughtful mood.

Thought I to myself, Oh, my God, he'll never speak to me again. He was expecting a good wrestle in the hay with one of these girls and he got nothing. He'll be so frustrated I'll hear about it at the studio for months to come.

Jimmy and Hank and I went over to him to offer him a drink to lift his spirits. "What's the matter, Bogey? Did you have a bad time?"

He looked up at us with the most profound emotion and said, "Anybody that would stick a cock in one of those girls would throw a rock through a Rembrandt."

When she told me this, I was a somewhat dumpy and mopey thirteen-year-old, and I thought it was the most exciting story I'd ever heard. It also made me depressed. Compared to my mother's early life, mine seemed unrelievedly bleak. With my unremarkable appearance, I felt I must be a big disappointment to her. My mother told me not to discuss her modeling days, because she said my father was jealous of her past and had burned all her scrapbooks.

The girls, or Voguettes, as they were called, were given drama lessons in hopes that a future star might emerge. My mother got a singing role in *Vogues of 1938*, but, since her voice was not her strong point, everyone sat around holding their ears. Jimmy Stewart was in the movie, and my mother went out with him. He was

World's Most Photographed Girls Make Their Debut in Hollywood

My mother in Hollywood as one of the Voguettes

very shy, and my mother thought of ways that might encourage him to kiss her. She decided that if she dropped her purse on the floor of his car and leaned down to pick it up, he might put his arm around her. It worked, and soon after, "The Kiss" happened. Now I wish I had asked for more details.

The Voguettes were invited to the opening of *Gone with the Wind*, and my mother borrowed a sweeping cape from the wardrobe department for the big night. As she walked onto the red carpet, the cape knocked over all the little flowerpots on the edge of the path.

My sister Lucinda recently sent me a copy of a letter our mother wrote to our grandmother from Hollywood in 1938. (As you can see, my mother ripped it up and threw it away shortly before she died. Lucinda rescued it and scotch-taped it back together.) Here's an excerpt:

> Gary Cooper was at Jimmy Stewart's and he's getting a divorce from his wife and someone says it's about time as she's so awful to him. Mother he is precious. Frank Shields was too attractive. His wife was with him

Mummy writes to her mother about adventures in Hollywood

and got too jealous as we played sardines and Frank and I were locked
in a closet by someone and they forgot to let us out so there we were for
about an hour. You should have seen the looks she gave me.

(Little wonder that Mrs. Shields was put out. Her husband was a noto-
rious ladies' man and a prodigious drinker. He had been an international tennis
star who had reached the finals at both Wimbledon and Forest Hills. He was not
yet thirty, but his partying had put his tennis career in sharp decline. He is now
chiefly remembered as Brooke Shields's grandfather.)

A publicity item about the Voguettes proved surprisingly prescient about
my mother's future: "'It isn't much fun when they tell you to walk and show your
dress off. Modeling taught me a great deal about myself, my good and bad points.'
She has no overwhelming ambition to be an actress. She wants to marry and have
kids. 'I'd like to marry a cave-man. I don't want to be pampered, bowed down to,
allowed to have my way all the time. You know, we models make good wives. A lot
of men are proud to be married to models. We are very domestic.' Olive has brown
hair and melting brown eyes. She looks the shyest, but is one of the most outspo-
ken. Height: 5 feet 6; weight, 120. Dress size, 12 to 14; bust, 34; waist, 25; hips, 35."
(My mother certainly got what she asked for in my father. It's also interesting how

My mother and father on a date at the Stork Club before he was sent overseas

different dress sizes were then. In later years, a size 12 to 14 would have swum on my mother, who was a modern size 8.)

My mother met my father in early 1939, on the eve of World War II. It was a blind date arranged by one of my father's friends from the Hun School in New Jersey. When the friend and his wife picked up Daddy at the Plaza Hotel, he saw an "astonishingly lovely girl" in the backseat. They were off to a weekend of skiing in Vermont, and Tom Watson and Olive Cawley talked without pause during the long drive. "I'd gone around with a lot of beautiful girls, but none of them had the unending generosity I found in her," he later wrote. "She was somewhat frivolous, but so was I." His parents hinted that they thought it unwise to date a model. "But I wanted somebody who would give me sweetness, love, and support." When Daddy spoke of my mother's sweetness, I wished that I could have experienced more of the sweetness he felt from her.

I have a photo of one of their early dates at the Stork Club. My father looks dashing in his uniform, and my mother has an orchid corsage pinned to her dress. Midway through the dinner my father invited my mother to go up in his plane, and they drove off to Teterboro Airport. He flew her over the brightly lit beautiful city, and then they returned to the Stork Club, resuming their dinner and dancing until the early hours of the new day.

My mother photographed in the dress she didn't get to wear at her wedding

My parents married hastily on a military base in Anniston, Alabama, shortly before my father was sent overseas. My mother never had a chance to wear her beautiful wedding dress, with her great-grandmother's lace veil, which was made by nuns in Brussels. My Watson grandparents were at the wedding, and my grandfather filled the tiny cottage where they spent their wedding night with beautiful flowers.

My parents had a lot in common and plenty of good times. They both loved to dance, sail, and ski, and they enjoyed their friends and family. The New York social scene was never of much interest to them.

But as my father wrote in his autobiography, they had a tempestuous marriage, which he blamed on his short temper. After suffering a heart attack in

1970, he became, by his own account, "self-absorbed, unappreciative, and rude." After going on a sail to Newfoundland, he returned to North Haven, and he and Mummy had a bitter fight. "I can't take this anymore," she said. "Fine," he replied, "I can't either."

He went out West with some friends, and she moved into a Manhattan apartment and hired a lawyer, ready for a divorce after thirty years of marriage. She refused to take my father's phone calls. When he and his sister, Helen, then took a trip to London, he suddenly felt faint and was hospitalized. He admitted the episode was "totally psychosomatic," but on returning to the States he had his secretary call my mother and tell her that he was seriously ill. She went right to his bedside, and within two days they were on their way to Europe — and to a reconciliation. I have inherited a beautiful pear-shaped diamond ring my father gave my mother when she returned. "Reports of our divorce are greatly exaggerated," he wired the IBM board.

When my mother was young, my grandfather bought her beautiful evening dresses from Dior. Later on she did not buy expensive clothes; her favorite store was Outdoor Traders on Greenwich Avenue. With her face and figure, everything she wore looked fabulous. One summer, she dazzled an editor from *Town & Country*, who went on to nominate her for the best-dressed list. When she was selected that fall, she told me that a few of her friends, who dressed only in couture, called to congratulate her in somewhat incredulous tones.

Mummy loved to give me advice on my dating life. To her, all relationships with men were based on a series of rules and game playing. One of her favorite sayings was, "Treat 'em mean and keep 'em keen." She practiced what she preached with my father, flirting and pouting and game playing, always withholding a bit of herself. When I married my second husband, Alex, and constantly showered him with praise, she pulled me aside and chastised me: "Don't say that — you'll spoil him!" I'm happy to say that I've spoiled him ever since.

My mother was adored by her grandchildren and loved gathering her family for dinner at the Big House. She told jokes and sometimes played Pass the Spoon. (To play Pass the Spoon, the initiator puts a tiny morsel of food on a spoon and passes to the next person who adds more. This continues until somebody spills and their penalty is to eat whatever is in the spoon). She was known for her generosity to her friends. And despite her occasional toughness with me, she showed me the same consideration. At lunch one day, as I was regaling her with stories about my

My mother in *Harper's Bazaar* in 1974, at age 55

recent studies with the Dalai Lama, she took off her beautiful pin, with the word Love written in exquisite little diamonds, and gave it to me.

She had a few mantras that kept her going. One was, "Laugh and the world laughs with you; cry and you cry alone." (This is certainly true for reasonably well-adjusted people, but not helpful to a depressed young daughter). She once recounted driving down Greenwich Avenue while weeping about something. She thought of her mantra and started laughing and drove home in a cheerful mood.

My mother liked light novels and wasn't interested in any sort of inner life. But she was a trouper as a corporate wife. She would go to endless IBM parties, always doing her best to charm people and reflect well on Daddy. She liked the kind of men she saw at these functions, big corporate honchos, guys who liked a drink and a good time. Even so, sometimes she found the party circuit boring, and my father had to remind her that IBM made our comfortable life possible, and she had no choice.

My mother's life took place largely in the car, ferrying us back and forth between our school and various appointments. In winters, her Fridays were pure hell. At four in the afternoon, she would pick up her six children at school and drive our blue Volkswagen van seven hours to Stowe. During the drive, my siblings and I fought, nagged, and cried. The constant question was, "How long 'til we get there?" In his book, my father said he used to drive up, too, but he must have been projecting. He always flew himself up and back in a small plane, sparing himself the challenging car ride.

My mother loved flirting and dancing and being the center of attention at parties. She'd have a couple of glasses of wine, and I'd see her gay, but not drunk. (My father had been a hard partier at Brown and frequented nightclubs in his early days at IBM. He continued to drink intermittently in the manner of men of his class and times, which was a good deal more than men do today.) Mummy could turn cartwheels until she was seventy, and danced the cha-cha with my brother at our annual square dance in North Haven until she was in her mid-seventies.

She also had a mischievous sense of humor. Once, when my father was having a reunion with his old army buddies at our Stowe house, she decided to surprise him. Imagining herself a kind of Irma La Douce, she bought a cheap, short, red-lace dress and a white-blond wig. She painted her face with lots of make-up and added false eyelashes. She traveled this way by plane to Burlington, Vermont — heaven knows what the other passengers thought — and when she arrived at our house in Stowe, my father hadn't a clue who she was.

My mother could also be quite ingenious and inventive in her problem solving. I remember that, for my seventh birthday, she wanted to show us cartoons. Alas, the projector didn't work: however she called their friend Chuck Percy, then CEO of Bell and Howell, later senator, and he was able to talk her through the process, and the party was a success!

She endured a two-year battle with cancer with nary a complaint and managed to look gorgeous while totally bald. During one of my visits with her at the Mayo Clinic, where she was being treated, I took her downstairs in her wheelchair to the incredibly dreary dining room, with many people in various stages of illness.

LEFT: My mother surprises my father
RIGHT: My mother shortly before the end: "I'm not dead yet."

Suddenly her face lit up. "*Now*, we're going to play a little game," she said. "We are going to decide who is attractive. For instance: the couple next to us is *not*." This kept her entertained until the end of dinner. I had to grin and bear it.

I can remember going to the emergency room with her when she was ill in her late eighties. As doctors gathered round, her eyes sparkled and she flirted like mad, charming them all. She kept her sense of humor until the end. My mother was in and out of the hospital a lot in her last few months and it was lucky there were six of us to share the caregiving. It was very healing for me to be involved with her care, as she was extremely appreciative and told me often that she loved me. I happened to be with her when she died, which was a profound experience. We had all been with my mother during the day, as she lay in a coma while Frank Sinatra's music, her favorite, played for hours. At night we took shifts ,and I took the first one. I was lying on her bed with my arm around her when the nurse woke me up and told me she had died. I felt terrible that I had been asleep when she died! My sister Olive was the last family member she spoke to. Twenty-four hours before dying, Mummy called Olive and said, amid laughter, "I'm not dead yet!"

Chapter Five

I attended the same school for eleven years, starting when I was three. Greenwich Country Day was prestigious, and all six of us eventually went there. My mother, or one of the other mothers in the carpool, would drive us there and back.

One of my early memories of school is swallowing a straight pin. It was St. Patrick's Day, and the teachers had cut out green paper shamrocks for all the pupils and had pinned them on our shirts. During our naptime I thought my pin looked as though it might be nice and cool in my mouth. I popped it in and shortly after it disappeared. I told the teacher that I might have swallowed a pin. The teacher dutifully attached a note with yet another straight pin, which read, "This child may have swallowed a pin." I was x-rayed and, yes, I had swallowed a pin. Poor Nanner had the unpleasant job of sifting through Big Job to make sure it came out.

First grade was momentous because it was the year I learned to read. Our first book was called *Johnny and Jenny Rabbit*. As my nickname was Jenny, I naturally felt it was about me. Once I started reading, there was no stopping me. I didn't just read books, I inhabited them. In my real life, I often felt lonely, despite being surrounded by five siblings. I often felt I had nothing in common with them or my parents and often wondered, hopefully, if I had been adopted and my real parents might be searching for me.

In the '50s, most kids had their tonsils out, almost as a rite of passage. In our family we were sent to the hospital in pairs. I went with Lucinda. She had a more difficult time following the surgery, and I remember a lot of medical equipment being brought in. I felt both relieved and guilty that it wasn't for me.

By second grade, school wasn't fun. I had a very strict teacher named Miss Molinari, and she didn't like my nervous habit of twisting my hair around my finger. Every time she saw me do it, she would make me stand in the corner. This made me so unhappy that one day I told my mother I didn't feel well and couldn't go to school. My mother cleverly asked where my stomach hurt. She later took me to the pediatrician who asked me the same question. I forgot the spot I'd told my mother and pointed somewhere else, at which point my bluff was called and back to school I went. No one ever thought of asking why I didn't want to go.

Greenwich Country Day was a school where physical discipline was part of the regimen. At a recent reunion, a classmate said in that, in third grade, one of the teachers shook him so hard that he passed out and woke up in the nurse's office. In fifth grade, another teacher used to put badly behaving students under his desk. It was rumored that he kicked them while they were down there. Our headmaster, John R. Webster, spanked a boy in front of our whole class for a bad report card. The teachers often threw erasers at students who were not paying attention. This sounds Dickensian now, but for us it was the norm. This was a time when adults were always right, and I think most parents felt that if their children were punished, it was because they deserved it.

The girls wore dresses, or skirts and blouses, knee socks, and Bass Weejuns. The boys wore button-down shirts with jackets, ties, and khaki pants.

We started each day with an assembly, a hymn, and a talk from our headmaster. If he noticed anyone whispering, he would make that student come up on stage and sing the hymn solo.

I was nine when my mother decided it was time to talk to me about sex. She led me to the back porch, off the living room, and shut the door. I believe she closed the curtains as well. First she asked if I knew anything about "the curse," as she called it. I lied and said no, not telling her about how, in the fourth grade, a delegation of three girls (myself included) snuck into the big girls' bathroom and opened up one of the little brown bags with a bloody Kotex inside. It looked horrible. My mother seemed relieved and explained about eggs and sperm, and gave me a book to read called *What's Happening to Me?* That was the extent of our discussion.

Mr. Webster always wore a beige three-piece suit, with a white carnation in his lapel, and was followed around by his black Standard Poodle. Each day before we went home, he shook hands with every student, and the girls were made to curtsey. Some of the kids loved the school, but I really hated it. Even the food was a source of misery. We had a seated hot lunch every day, served by our teacher at tables of ten. I can still see the boiled, soggy broccoli, grisly meat, and watery mashed potatoes made from a mix. Once we were served, the teacher often made me stay until I finished, reminding me how lucky I was and insisting that my next school would not have such good food.

By the time I reached sixth grade, there was a hierarchy in the class as rigid as that in the court of Louis XIV. Suddenly, girls who had been my friends seemed to gravitate more towards the cooler, more popular students. This was very painful, and I felt myself growing more isolated and retreating more and more into my beloved world of books.

As the class went into puberty there began to be more pairing off between the boys and the girls. The classroom was ripe with awakening sexuality. I remember the boys touching the girl's backs to see if they were wearing bras. I was so grateful I was wearing one the day some boy checked me out!

The school day is like a workday: If you hate school or work, the hours stretch on for an eternity. Over fifty years later, I still rejoice that I don't have to go to Greenwich Country Day or play field hockey or go to dancing class. No inmate was happier getting out of jail than I was leaving that school.

Around this time, I remember my mother eying me appraisingly, the way one might a prize Doberman Pinscher. She said, "Your father and I are thinking of having your ears pinned back. One of the Jones twins just had it done."

My ears? A whole new thing to worry about... Did they stick out too much? I studied them again and again. Ultimately my parents decided not to go ahead with the surgery.

From sixth through eighth grade, I kept a journal in which each page was divided into three sections, to make room for each of the three years. Around twenty years ago, I looked back at that journal and burned it, hoping to obliterate the unhappy memories of those years. Each day in the journal was a litany of misery. Sometimes I hated my mother and various siblings; I felt I had no one to talk to at home or at school. The isolation increased when my mother did imitations of my best friend, who was extremely shy. In order to avoid my mother's imitations, I stopped inviting my friend over.

In those days, depression wasn't a major concern the way it is now, and many parents and educators scarcely recognized it as a real illness, especially in young girls. But I didn't need a psychological diagnosis to know that I was sad all the time, often crying and wishing I were dead. One of my younger sisters once came to my room and found me outside my third-floor window on a freezing winter day, sitting on the small ledge with no clothes on. "What are you doing?" she asked. "I'm sitting here so I can get pneumonia and die," I responded melodramatically. At that point I couldn't imagine a happy future. I even remember trying to strangle myself with my hands, but it hurt too much! I wasn't getting along with my mother or my siblings. In families, kids often get labeled—the pretty one, the smart one, the athletic one. I, sadly, didn't fit into any of these positive categories and was known more as the inept one. My mother was so quick and efficient that she was often irritated by my clumsy way of doing things, which made my ineptness part of a vicious cycle. Often she couldn't resist clicking her tongue against her teeth in exasperation, making a noise that sounded like "Sta"—followed by an irritated sigh, "hahh."

Because no one thought I was capable, when I took my driver's license test, no one asked if I passed. Even I was amazed that I had passed! Actually, it was amazing that I did pass! I can still remember the sunny day of my test. When the instructor asked me to make a left turn, I did, and I accidently turned on the windshield wipers and couldn't figure out how to turn them off! I completed the test with wipers flapping wildly, while I pretended nothing was wrong.

Dancing classes started in the sixth grade and were held every Friday afternoon after school. All the girls brought suitcases to school, packed with their party dresses, white gloves, and black patent-leather party shoes; the boys were already wearing jackets and ties. Some of the mothers would come to school to help their daughters get dressed. One classmate had long braids that her mother would ceremoniously unplait, brushing out her beautiful long wavy hair. Dressed in our party frocks, fancy shoes, and white socks, we were herded into the gym, where the boys were waiting. We would stand in a circle—alternating boy, girl, boy, girl—and Miss Hallowell, wearing a lovely long dress and holding a clicker, would instruct us. She clicked the clicker to get our attention and then, accompanied only by a pianist, she would demonstrate dances. We did the foxtrot, the lindy, the bunny hop, the cha-cha, the waltz, and the Mexican Hat Dance. She had the boys rotate partners between each dance.

The greatest indignity for me was "boy's choice." The girls would sit in a circle around the dance floor and wait to be chosen. Inevitably there were always about three extra girls who would have to sit out the entire dance, trying not to look too unhappy. The time spent sitting out a dance with no partner seemed like an eternity, and I remember my face burning with humiliation. My mother, an authority on popularity, would say, "Smile! Look like you're having a good time." I would think, "Great—in addition to being unpopular, I will look crazy for being so happy about it!" Sometimes the humiliation was even worse, as the mothers would sit and watch the class. I couldn't wait to go home for Friday night hamburgers and French fries, followed by *77 Sunset Strip*.

School was a special agony from seventh to ninth grades. I sink into a black hole just thinking about those years: the humiliation on the hockey field, when teams were chosen and I was often the last to be picked; the group showers after sports, a torture for painfully modest me. I became more and more attached to my own suffering. My academics were extremely undistinguished, to say the least, and by ninth grade I was failing math and science.

Also in ninth grade, it became the fad for mothers to take their daughters to the beauty parlor for a "permanent." My hair was naturally wavy, but nevertheless my mother took me to the hairdresser. To add to the indignity of the permanent wave, the hairdresser cut my bangs too short. I wept when I saw my frizzy hair and unflattering bangs.

Strangely enough, good grades, particularly among the girls, were not really valued in our family. Because my grandfather had barely finished high school and my father had repeated two years, I guess Daddy felt that stellar academic records weren't really necessary for a successful life.

Divorce was becoming common in Greenwich in the '50s. Our neighbor, who often drove us to school and who usually looked quite sour, was suddenly singing romantic show tunes in the car and looking happier than ever. Shortly after, we were stunned to learn that she had been having an affair and was divorcing her husband.

Hearing about this was heavy stuff for me. I was also revolted by it, being quite puritanical. When I was thirteen, my mother talked to me about men who "strayed," as though it were a natural part of every marriage. Greenwich truly seemed a kind of Peyton Place. Many of the couples who were friends of my parents were living secret lives. Or sometimes not so secret: The father of one of my dearest friends flagrantly parked his car in the driveway of his lover.

By about age twelve, many of the kids at Greenwich Country Day had paired off into romantic couples. I did not have a boyfriend and would hear wistfully about the make-out parties that I was missing. I also heard about games like Spin the Bottle. I dreaded dancing class and longed to be away in a place where I didn't have to see boys. For some reason I found them terrifying, although I did develop crushes on some. After a party in Stowe, at the advanced age of fifteen, I practically burst into tears when a boy tried to kiss me.

Our property was large enough that I could disappear for hours. I used to climb up in a tall pine tree with a book and sit there, totally hidden, ignoring the governess calling my name. I have never again been able to read with the total abandon of my young self. At ten, I read *Gone with the Wind*, which transported me. I spent the weekend immersed in the lives of Scarlett and Rhett, distracted from my dreary existence. Before that, I loved reading fantasy books. *The Wonderful Wizard of Oz* enchanted me.

I later took a course with Jean Houston, a legendary spiritual teacher. In one class she focused on Dorothy's heroic journey in the movie *The Wizard of Oz*. Dorothy finds allies — the Cowardly Lion, the Scarecrow, and the Tin Man — who help her on her soul's journey towards a glorious Technicolor universe, away from the black-and-white conventional world of Kansas. On the way to Oz, Dorothy matures as she overcomes obstacles and develops inner wisdom — the sacred potential in all of us — and opens her heart to community and friendship. The song "Somewhere over the Rainbow" expresses her yearning for a different, more spiritual life. I yearned for that life as well.

Peter Pan was another favorite. I used to dream that Peter would visit me at night and teach me to fly and take me to Neverland. *Mary Poppins* and Hans Christian Andersen's fairy tales helped prepare me for the difficulties of life. *Mary Poppins* was alternately frightening and sad — as well as magical and shamanic. I love this passage, from *Mary Poppins Comes Back*, in which Annabel, a baby, is speaking to a wise starling:

"I am earth and air and fire and water," she said softly. "I come from the Dark where all things have their beginning.... I come from the sea and its tides.... I come from the sky and its stars, I come from the sun and its brightness....And

I come from the forests of earth.... Slowly I moved at first... always sleeping and dreaming."

She ends with: "It was a long journey."

The plot of one Hans Christian Andersen story especially haunted me. A king, after the death of his wife, remarries an evil stepmother, who turns his eleven boy children into swans. Their sister desperately wants to rescue them and is told by a witch that the only way she can do this is by not speaking until she weaves eleven shirts out of nettles (which painfully prick her fingers) and throws them over the swans.

In the meantime, a prince falls in love with the princess and marries her, even though she cannot speak. As time goes by, she is denounced as a witch and sentenced to burning, but she never stops making the shirts. Just before she is to be burned, the swans fly down and she throws the shirts on them. Miraculously, they all become human again, and she's able to speak and declare her innocence. After much pain and suffering, all is well. Somehow I identified with this heroine, as my shyness often rendered me mute. Perhaps I felt that, one day, I would be able to speak and be able to help my siblings and others.

(Andersen often lived out his life and fantasies through his tales. A young friend recently pointed out to me that his heroines often die young and virginal, so they can't be corrupted by sex. Brought up in extreme poverty, he was humiliated that his mother was an alcoholic and his aunt ran a brothel. He was never able to have the happy home life he dreamed of, and he struggled with homosexual desires. He must have felt that he suffered as much as those eleven brothers and their silent sister.)

Reading Alcott's *Little Women*, I identified with Jo's depression and rage at her younger sister Amy, even though I felt I had more in common with Meg, who longed for marriage and children. The eponymous Jane Eyre, mousy and plain, was another favorite –and, dear reader, she did find love and happiness despite many adversities, though of course her prince had to be maimed and blinded before she could be married. When I was about ten, I started reading Anya Seton's historic novels. I found them quite erotic, with bodices ripping and breasts heaving.

Joan of Arc was also a fascinating heroine, led by her mysterious voices and psychic powers. I adored Frances Hodgson Burnett and wanted to be like Sara Crewe in *A Little Princess*. I hoped I would have the courage to behave like a princess, no matter what the circumstances. Burnett's book *The Secret Garden* contains wonderful insights into the power of thought, which may have subliminally been a lesson for me:

> In each century since the beginning of the world wonderful things have been discovered. In the last century more amazing things were found out than in any century before....One of the new things people began to find out in the last century was that thoughts—just mere thoughts— are as powerful as electric batteries—as good for one as sunlight is, or as bad for one as poison. To let a sad thought or a bad one get into your mind is as dangerous as letting a scarlet fever germ get into your body...

Later on in this passage, Burnett writes of a major character: "When new, beautiful thoughts begin to push out the old, hideous ones, life begins to come back and strength pours in like a flood."

My grandfather felt that every house should have a "gentleman's library" of the classics (most of which he had never read), and he gave my parents yards of books for their new home. The volumes were bound in beautiful red leather, embossed with gold, and displayed proudly on the wall of our library, where no one touched them. While browsing, one day, at the age of ten, I came across the first sentence of *Vanity Fair*: I was instantly hooked and removed the three volumes from the sacred library. My mother saw one volume carelessly open on my bed, and both parents gave me a lecture on respect for the books. Becky Sharpe and Amelia Sedley were removed from my room and returned to the library, never to leave again.

I read so fast that my mother couldn't believe I was absorbing what I read. She once quizzed me on a book I was reading and was surprised to find that I could remember everything. This ability to read quickly was a great benefit to me, later, as a bookseller. I could take home a pile of books and—even without reading them in their entirety—get a good sense of them and know which to recommend to which customers.

Apart from my beloved books, the great solace during these years was my friend Siri and her mother, Pat Larsen. When my father built the family house in Stowe, in 1957, the Larsens were our next-door neighbors. Siri, the oldest, was my age, followed closely by four younger brothers, and the two families became great friends. It turned out that Siri and her mother were avid readers, and we loved to talk about what we were reading. I adored Mrs. Larsen, who was very differ-ent from my parents' other friends. She was a wonderful artist, and her watercolor landscapes still adorn the walls of our house in Stowe. She also wrote haikus, was friends with *New Yorker* critic Brendan Gill, and even attended Truman Capote's famous Black and White Ball. She seemed to live in an entirely different, and more interesting, universe from most of the people I knew.

Mrs. Larsen had high cheekbones, large brown eyes, long, graying hair worn up in various hairdos, and golden skin that bronzed easily, like her lovely daughter Siri's. She was extremely unconventional and would invite guests to take a sauna with her and then roll naked around in the snow to cool off. She had a marvelous sense of humor, and we were often amused by the same things. Mrs. Larsen intro-duced us to the books of Mazo de la Roche, a well-regarded Canadian author. We all loved her *Jalna* series, about the Whitehead family: fifteen novels that spanned a hundred-year period. The series' length was great for me, as I could disappear into the lives of the Whiteheads for a long time, despite being a fast reader.

Mrs. Larsen would also console me when I confessed to her and Siri how miserable I was: She told me that things would improve (which, in time, they did). "You are a late bloomer," she said. "One day you will be much happier." This meant a lot to me and gave me hope for the future.

Chapter Six

Wꜞhen I was ten, I took my first big trip, flying to Paris with my mother and father. Travelling alone with my parents was an exciting experience. My parents later told me that they took me out of school to cheer me up, as I seemed a bit sad. My grandfather's death had been a big shock to me, even though he had been ill. His very existence had served as a protective cape around me. I recall Nanner weeping and telling me the news, while I stood too numb to weep: that came later...

My psychiatrist and I later figured out that this was when sadness started to envelope me like a thick Maine fog. To lose the one person who adored me and made me feel special was a huge blow. My parents believed in the power of the individual to straighten up and fly right. Their mantra was, "When the going gets tough, the tough get going." They also said, "It's hard, but it's fair." These maxims didn't work for me. I think I would have benefited greatly from going to a good therapist, an energy healer, and a different school.

All my life I have kept journals intermittently, and I still have the diary from this Paris trip. My old diary—in beautiful brown leather with gold embossing, now a bit faded around the edges—says *Travels* across the front. Each day I wrote the date, and the rest of the page was devoted to remarks. At the end of the first page, I wrote, "I can't wait to go to sleep because mummy and I are sleeping together. Good night."

In the diary's "autograph" section, I collected the signatures of the pilot and all the stewardesses. I was even allowed to sit in the copilot's seat. Under "incidents," my father wrote, "On our way to Paris all the European Airports were locked in and we had to return to Gander which made us five hours late arriving in Paris."

I have always loved to travel, and I think it is partly because my father was an intrepid globetrotter and often took us along. This Paris trip was partly business for my father, who visited various IBM people. I was struck by the grandeur of the city, my favorite still. My journal records our blissful arrival at the Ritz: "We had tea and went to bed. The sheets were woven of linen and I slept well." Oh, those sheets! Their cool smoothness was so unlike the regular sheets at home.

I went shopping with my mother, and she bought me a blue taffeta dress with a lace collar. I also accompanied my mother to my first fashion show at Christian Dior. I was fascinated by the tall, elegant models walking with their pelvises thrust forward and their heads back. I later entertained my parents at the Ritz by imitating their gliding motion. At night I was cared for by a Madam Peelyvweet (my ten-year-old spelling—I haven't a clue as to real one). My introduction to art occurred at the Louvre, where I saw the Winged Victory and a statue of Diana and the Venus de Milo. (My astute critical judgment of the Mona Lisa: "She looks like a witch!")

We also visited Amsterdam, Brussels, and England. While in England we went to Stratford-upon-Avon, and my parents took me to see *Macbeth* with Laurence Olivier and Vivien Leigh. I was riveted by their stage presence and masterful soliloquies. Since then I have seen *Macbeth* on numerous occasions, but I have never been to a performance as electrifying as that one. After the show, my parents and I stayed at a spooky manor house, and I had nightmares about the witches.

When I was twelve, my father took all of us except Susan and Helen to the Brussels World's Fair. We went around in something called a *pousse-pousse*, a kind of basket where you sat in front of a motorcycle. We visited all the pavilions, starting with IBM's. There, we were impressed by a machine that could translate any word into French. In the Russian pavilion, we saw a statue of Stalin, as well as the Sputnik satellite that had taken a dog into space. The American pavilion was huge, one of the biggest circular buildings in the world, complete with two redwood trees. Daddy insisted on taking us downtown to see the famous statue of the little boy peeing, Manneken-Pis — much to our embarrassment.

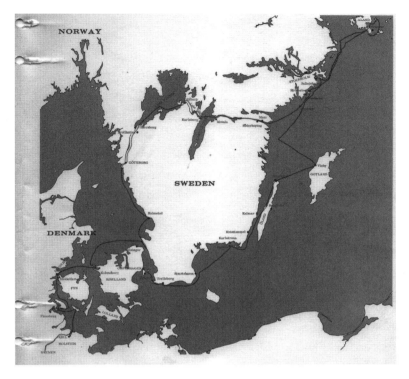

Our trip in Scandinavia in 1958. We covered a lot of water.

My parents were invited to the palace and had lunch with King Baudouin, ex-King Leopold, and his wife, Princess Liliane. We proceeded to Holland and then to Bremen, Germany, where we visited Abeking and Rasmussen, the boat builders who had created the second *Palawan*. The first *Palawan*, a fifty-one-foot sloop, was built in 1951 and sold six years later because our family had outgrown it. That summer, we took the new fifty-eight-foot yawl on a tour of Scandinavia.

After extensive research and conversation with sailor friends, my father came up with an ambitious itinerary: Start from Bremen...Passage through the Kiel Canal...Up through the Danish Islands to Copenhagen...North to Oslo...Back to Göteborg on the west coast of Sweden...Through the Gota Canal, which traverses the heartland of the Swedish countryside to Stockholm...North from Stockholm and east to Mariehamn in the Aland Islands...Further east to Helsinki...Back down to Visby on Gotland Island...Down the east and southern coast of Sweden, ending up in Copenhagen.

As travel was still quite special in those days, my father sent his four daughters (baby Helen stayed at home) and my mother corsages to wear on this trip. My grandmother came to the airport to see us off. People dressed for travel as they would for church. No blue jeans or leisure suits allowed. The stewardesses were all young, slender, and beautiful, wearing fitted suits and shoes with heels.

I had been dreading the trip. At age twelve, I couldn't imagine anything worse than sleeping with three young sisters in the main cabin of our boat. My brother, the only boy, always had his own room, as, of course, did my parents. Our German captain, Paul Walter, slept in the crew's quarters. We sailed off into a terrible storm (which my father must have loved), and I wrote in my diary, "Everybody was throwing up, but not me."

All the places we cruised in Scandinavia were very safe, so once Palawan was tied up at the dock, we kids would go off on our own. We wandered around old towns, and went to ancient castles, and old-fashioned one-ring circuses. Going through the Kiel Canal was an adventure. We had two bikes on board and could ride alongside the boat. At one point, Olive, Lucinda, and I went out to explore Kiel, and we lost Lucinda. Olive and I tried to find her and got lost ourselves. All of us eventually found our way back, and our parents didn't seem terribly concerned. They felt somehow we would all be safe, and that was great for us, as we had a lot of freedom. It rained many times that summer, but we had just discovered the game Monopoly and spent hours playing. Elvis Presley was big that summer, too, and I can remember getting off the boat and hearing groups of young people singing "Love Me Tender."

Our whole family was impressed with the Swedes' casualness about nudity. My father and brother, Tom, used binoculars to admire sunbathers as our boat glided by. In Saltsjöbaden, Sweden, my mother took us swimming, and, in the women's changing room, the woman in charge had nothing on but a whistle.

I look back in awe at how my mother managed to cope with five children and a caveman for the summer. Not only did she do most of the cooking, she did our laundry by hand, putting it out to dry around the railing of the boat—much to my father's dismay. Captain Walter would occasionally cook German sausage, served with hash browns fried with onions and bacon. I still cook this dish for my youngest son, Matthew.

When I was thirteen, my parents thought it would be nice for me to improve my French by living with a French family. They found the family through an IBM connection in Paris. Again, my parents took me to Paris, and we luxuriated at the Ritz. We ran into Rose Kennedy, who was in Paris to see the couture collections, so that she could plan her fall wardrobe. I remember her in a beautiful red suit, with hair immaculately coiffed and heavily sprayed. She and my mother knew each other from the days when Mummy dated her son Jack, and she joined us for tea at the Ritz. I then met the family I would be staying with: the Count and the Countess de Gourcuff. I drove with them to a chalet in Méribel les Allues, in Savoie, where I stayed for a month. I felt lonely at first, but soon fell in with the rhythms of my French family. Here is an entry from my diary at the time:

> I'm not as homesick as I was. I guess it's because Mme de Gourcuff is so nice to me, she treats me just like a daughter. The boy, Patrick, is so polite to me you'd think I was the Queen of Sheba. He says he's sorry for things he didn't do...

> I have forgotten to describe Lulu, the most important character of all. Lulu is the dog. He is not very big, and I'm not sure what I'm doing telling that he's a shambergel but that's what Marcella says he is. He is very warm and lovable. Children are his people. He came from a farmer who, to me, looked like a perfect French Farmer with round jolly face and pink cheeks.

> We certainly have delicious meals here. We have our big meal in the middle of the day. First we have shredded carrot and tomatoes or something like that for our hors d'oeuvre then we have meat and potatoes, then salad, after we have cheese, bread and last but not least, our fruits. For supper we have potage, and then some cold meat and salad, then breads, cheese and then some delicious desserts.

> I have just finished Jamaica Inn by Daphne du Maurier. Besides having such a lovely name she writes with genius. She always springs such surprises on you. I was horrified when the albino priest turned out to be the leader of the wreckers! But all is well that ends well!

~

Leaving for our trip out West, with our pilot dressed for work
(From left: Lucinda, Olive, and me)

The next summer my father decided to fly us all out West. He had a small Aero Commander that was like a bucking bronco in the wind. I remember him flying us over the Grand Canyon (saying, excitedly, "Look at the Grand Canyon!") as he zoomed along—ignoring, or not noticing, that the plane was bouncing wildly.

In the back of the plane, my mother was holding airsick bags for two of her children, who missed the Grand Canyon entirely. When we arrived, my youngest sister's outfit was covered with the contents of her stomach. My mother, most inventively, had Helen remove her pants and step into the sleeves of her sweater, giving her a chic pantaloon look right out of *The King and I*. After viewing the Grand Canyon, we spent the night at a nearby lodge. Several glasses of wine at dinner helped convince Daddy that this was the ideal time to teach me how to drive.

We proceeded to the pitch-dark parking lot and got into a stick-shift car. I sat terrified as my father explained gear shifts, etc. After he finished, he said, "I will hold my hand up and hit your knee whenever you make a mistake, and that will help you remember." Needless to say, this was not helpful, and I remember that

Watson family reunion at the Valley Ranch.
I am the first on the left in the second row. (photo by Toni Frissell)

nighttime drive over hilly roads as the trip from hell! I didn't attempt driving for six more years. I finally got my license at eighteen.

On that same trip, we had a Watson family reunion at the Valley Ranch in Cody, Wyoming. I developed a crush on a very handsome teenager who delivered ice to the room every afternoon. I would race back to the cabin so I could be there when my heartthrob arrived—he would wittily announce himself saying "The Iceman cometh."

Somehow I don't recollect as much tension when we were on these trips. Perhaps my father was calmer being away from the stress of the office. He didn't have to witness at-home irritants such as extra mail on the hall table, which always set him off. I remember these trips as the happiest times with both my parents.

Chapter Seven

I was extremely happy to close the book on my life at Greenwich Country Day School and start a new chapter at Miss Hall's, an all-girls boarding school founded in 1898. My mother drove me to Pittsfield, Massachusetts, where my new life would start.

The main part of the school was in a large brick Georgian building with white columns that sat atop a gently rising hill with a circular driveway. A large, dramatic entryway gave way to a double staircase directly across from the front door. The staircase led up to the second and third floors, where our bedrooms were. I was put in a bedroom for three, and, after my mother helped me unpack, I was left alone, terrified and shy.

I was repeating the ninth grade, because I hadn't completed the math and science requirements at Greenwich Country Day. Even so, I was not the oldest in the class and was still quite immature. The freshman class was small—only around 20 of us in a school of 130 girls. Gradually, I began to relax, in what seemed to me to be a nurturing atmosphere, and the happier I felt, the better I performed academically. I enjoyed the cloistered environment in the Berkshires, where I rarely had to see boys. Since we all wore incredibly ugly uniforms, there was no competition over clothes, I didn't need to worry that Wynne Dewart had more straight skirts than I did. We were not allowed to wear slacks. Shortly after the school year started, we had to give a book report. One of the "girls" told me recently, at our

Approaching the main building at Miss Hall's School

fiftieth reunion, that she'd asked me what she should read for the report. "Read *Wuthering Heights*," I'd answered. "It's my favorite book."

The school had extremely strict rules. Before we arrived, we were sent a booklet that spelled them out for us. No chewing gum. No walking barefoot in the halls. No visiting after lights out. As well as the obvious: no sex, no alcohol, no drugs. Even when we sunbathed on the lawn behind the school, we were required to wear modest one-piece bathing suits. We blithely lathered ourselves with baby oil and iodine, with nary a thought of future skin cancer. We even created sun reflectors out of tinfoil. One of my classmates ingeniously got around the bathing-suit rule by cutting out a flap in the middle of her suit, so she could get a bikini tan but could quickly pull the flap over if a teacher walked by.

Boys –at least, boys "understood" to be known to our parents—could visit the school "on Saturday or Sunday afternoons when there is generally enough 'tea' to feed the man, and when you may have him as your guest in the living room or, within bounds, on campus. Always remember to introduce him to the teacher on duty who is the hostess of the afternoon, and if you go out for a walk, let her know that you can be found within walking distance of the house…Your guest, if it is a 'he,' does not go into any part of the school other than the living room—please remember this!"

Miss Hall's had a dark, Orwellian side too. Both the administration and some class officers spied on the girls. We had an honor code and were required to sign in every week with a plus or minus, depending on whether we had broken the rules. I usually gave myself a plus, despite having committed a few minor sins, such as walking barefoot in the hall or chewing gum. When one classmate gave herself a plus, a student-council member asked her to reconsider. Hadn't she sung "Who's Afraid of the Big Bad Wolf?" after lights-out? Another former student recently told me that Miss Fitch—our dreaded headmistress—called her into her office to lecture her on the evils of Tampax (somehow she knew which of us had the vile habit). Miss Fitch claimed that Tampax was a substitute for sex, and that was why the girls used it. I guess she felt Kotex was more ladylike—less penetrating.

Once, in my junior year, all students were summoned to the gymnasium for a special meeting. The doors were shut, and we waited expectantly for a heinous denouement, racking our brains for sins we might have committed. Miss Fitch, at her most forbidding, stood and said, "Girls, something terrible has happened! Something so terrible I have sent our English boarding student out of the room." She paused dramatically as we waited in eager anticipation to hear the atrocity. In tones of indignation and horror, she said, "Someone has put lemon peels on the cross in the meditation room."

A stunned silence followed, and then Miss Fitch added, "We know who did this, and I will wait for you to turn yourself in after this meeting." With that, the meeting ended, and we were all left to wonder who the perpetrator was. Whoever did it saw through Miss Fitch's bluff, and the mystery persists to this very day.

We had several study periods a day, in between classes, which were held in different rooms in the same building. I would race through my work, sign out for the library, and immerse myself in books. I read novels ravenously, moving alphabetically from Jane Austen to the Brontes, and so on. Then I started in on the drama section, reading plays by William Inge and Tennessee Williams, among others. Later I became hooked on Rasputin, reading everything I could find about him. I was fascinated by photos of him, with his smoldering dark eyes, surrounded by his female followers. Lawrence of Arabia thrilled me, and I was entranced by his *Seven Pillars of Wisdom*. I'm too embarrassed to say how many times I saw the movie with Peter O'Toole in the title role. As usual, I had two lives—my actual life and my virtual life in books. Reading was a great escape and took me out of myself and into another world: a better world, where I didn't worry about anything. The time would fly by, and I was totally content all by myself.

I enjoyed the peacefulness and predictability of the school's regimented days. Contrary to what the teachers at Greenwich Country Day had told me, the food was delicious. At night, we ate at tables of ten, headed by a teacher or senior, with girls taking turns as waiters. We would have meals similar to what I had at home: a roast, potatoes, and vegetables, followed by dessert (the chocolate soufflé was particularly memorable). Lunch was buffet-style, with lots to choose from. Twice a year we signed up for Girl Scout cookies, sometimes ordering and devouring huge amounts. Many of the girls—myself included—became a bit overweight, much to my mother's dismay. I came down with pneumonia my junior year and consequently lost about fifteen pounds. My mother and I were both ecstatic, and I can still remember the patchwork madras slacks she bought me as a reward.

On Saturdays, the big treat was to be bussed into the center of Pittsfield, where we could wander around and shop. Because our allowances were set by the school and quite puny, I restricted my shopping to food and especially movie magazines. I avidly followed the turbulent love lives of the stars—Debbie and Eddie, then Elizabeth and Eddie, and finally Richard and Elizabeth. What a romantic merry-go-round. I was fascinated by the Old World glamour of the stars, who all seemed to wear fur coats with dark glasses and splashy jewels. Debbie, Doris, Elizabeth, and Audrey would never have wandered around in sweats, as our disheveled leading ladies do now. Cary Grant always looked debonair. Years ago, my son Ralph and I were walking along Fifth Avenue when we saw him coming toward us on the sidewalk. He was perfectly tanned, soigné, and one of the handsomest men I have ever seen.

While in Pittsfield I bought Callard & Bowser licorice, then headed off to Friendly's, where I had a sublime hamburger topped off with a butterscotch sundae. I recently attended my fiftieth reunion and was hoping to duplicate my Friendly's experience. Sadly, the restaurant no longer serves butterscotch, only caramel—not at all the same thing.

Back at school, I would curl up on my bed and eat licorice while perusing the movie magazines. I even read *True Confessions*, which featured tales of girls surrendering their virtue to all manner of cads. It seemed quite racy then, but was very tame by today's standards.

All dressed up in my Sunday best

On Saturday nights, we were shown movies such as *Gigi* or *Carousel*, and I learned the words to all the songs. Sundays were less fun, because a lot of the day was taken up by church, which was mandatory. We started out with a chapel service at the school. Then buses would appear in the driveway, and off we'd go to services in Pittsfield, dressed in suits, stockings, heels, gloves, and hats. I do not remember any great sermons, but I loved the hymns, which I knew from Greenwich Country Day assemblies and from going to church with my family. We would return later for a formal lunch, and by then it seemed the weekend was over, because we had a 5:00 p.m. study hall. Several times a year, we were excused from church for a "sleepover." This meant we could sleep late and come to the dining room in our bathrobes and eat sticky buns.

At our fiftieth reunion, I sat next to a woman who told me that she'd wanted to go to church on those Sundays, while the rest of us slept in, and had asked one of the heads of the school if she could. This created quite a kerfuffle and prompted the headmistress to call her parents to suggest that perhaps Miss Hall's was not the school for her. Later they worked out a solution to this vexing problem, and she was able to attend church while the rest of us happily slept late.

Miss Fitch was rather stout. You always knew when she was coming up behind you in study hall, because her legs, encased in stockings, would rub together and create a swishing sound. She lived with the academic director, Miss Ellis, and, at the time, nobody thought anything of their relationship. I stayed off their radar, which was fine with me.

The third in the ruling triumvirate was Miss Witherspoon. She seemed ancient to me, at the time, though I have no idea how old she was—as Auntie Mame would say, "Somewhere between forty and death." Every year she told the senior class the sad story of how her fiancé was killed in the First World War (which does give a clue about her age). She was concerned about our spiritual development, and every night at the end of study hall she would read aloud a passage from the Bible. The passage was repeated each night for a week, and on Sunday evening, we had to write it from memory.

Before our spring dance, we would meet to discuss how the party should proceed. Miss Witherspoon would sit in stately splendor on one of the sofas in the living room, flanked by the school president, the head of Student Council, and other dignitaries. The hoi polloi would sit on the floor, gazing at Miss Witherspoon with rapt attention.

She would always start out by saying, in her Southern accent, "Now, girls, let us *visualahhs* [visualize]. The *boas* [boys] will arrive on the bus—be met *bah* [by] the committee and taken to the gym *wheah* [where] they will be given their dance cards. Each *boa* will find their partner for the evening." Partners were always selected by height, and my friend Prudy Painter (now Freyberger), at five foot two, was always paired with the tiniest boy. I loved the dance cards, because they meant I always had a partner, and there were often extra boys to cut in. One danced with one's partner during the first, middle, and final dances. The other dancers on the cards were all filled in with different names, so no one was left sitting mournfully on the sidelines.

"No one will leave the gym or be seen walking with a *boa*. We expect you to act like ladies!" Before the dances, there were dress inspections. I can remember Miss Witherspoon sitting on a bench on the landing of the first floor with the school president and head of student council. In our dresses, girdles (which even the thinnest girls wore), stockings, and heels, we would parade in front of them so they could make sure our dresses were not too provocative. If Miss Witherspoon (or "Withy," as we privately called her) felt the dress was too short, one had to kneel in front of her to see if the dress hit the floor. If it didn't, the dress did not pass. Often after these "inspections," the girls would shorten their dresses or create a more revealing neckline.

At Miss Hall's, the spring dance was compulsory, and the rest were optional. My attitude about these social encounters was theatrically summed up in a letter to my mother during my senior year: "We have the Deerfield Dance tomorrow night. Ugh—quelle horreur! Trying to make conversation with some stupid boy who has a 98 i.q., a face like Frankenstein and various other deformities." Even so, my mother bought me the most beautiful dress for the occasion—shocking-pink taffeta, sleeveless, and tea-length. It was very fitted, buttoned down the back with covered buttons, and stayed fitted until a bit below the waist, where it became fuller and tied with a sash. I think it was designed by Oleg Cassini. I was thrilled when my mother told me she had seen Jackie Kennedy in an identical dress at a White House party.

In retrospect, it is amazing my mother bought me such an extravagant dress, as she was usually quite frugal. When her daughters were at Greenwich Country Day, she would buy each of us two new outfits every autumn, and we all felt terribly deprived. We were always telling her, "I need it for school," and my sisters and I still joke to each other when we buy something, saying, "I needed it for school." Of course, one of the benefits of being the oldest is that I didn't have to wear hand-me-downs.

One of our best dances was on Father's Day. The fathers would play a game of softball with us, and then we would prepare for the dance. I was always excited about these evenings, because my father was one of the most popular dads. Before the dance started, we would link arms with our fathers and sing, "My Heart Belongs to Daddy."

One girl gazed at my father for two years in rapt, almost tearful admiration before she had the nerve to cut in (as we all did during this event). As she was dancing with him, she had an ecstatic expression on her face. Another friend gave my father one of his most prized compliments: "Mr. Watson, you are the *sexiest* father at the Father's Day dance!" In fact, all the fathers seemed handsome and charming, and they could dance well, which was a relief after getting our toes crushed by some of the oafs from the boys' schools.

~

My generation grew up in fear of the atom bomb. At school we had drills in which we would leave our classrooms and kneel in the halls, face down, with our hands over our heads. A lot of people had bomb shelters built adjacent to their homes, my family included. We had two, one in Greenwich and one in Stowe.

In Greenwich, our bomb shelter was located in our large basement, which also housed the laundry room. I remember walking past the huge machines, smelling the damp, clean clothes (and with six children there were always mountains of laundry, some of it hanging up to dry, attached to the line by clothespins). There was a way of entering the bomb shelter through a zigzag passage in the basement, similar to entering an Egyptian tomb. Once inside, the rather small shelter had twelve bunk beds, enough for our family and the household staff. There was a toilet and electricity, which was somehow produced by riding a stationary bike. We had a small kitchen area and a store of very unappetizing canned food, as well as some books (one of which, aptly enough, was *Gone with the Wind*). Daddy even conducted some drills in which the older girls would each collect a younger sister from school and run home with them to the bomb shelter.

There were also guns, which we would use to shoot the neighbors if they tried to get in, as the shelter only had food and water for our household. I couldn't figure out which was worse — suffering the effects of the bomb, or being confined in that bleak space with my family, taking potshots at neighbors. During this period I read *On the Beach* and had recurring nightmares of living in a post-apocalyptic world.

Daddy felt that, if there was a nuclear attack, Stowe would be the safest spot for us. Since I was at Miss Hall's during this period, Daddy gave me an envelope with one hundred dollars in cash and told me that, if I thought we were in danger of an attack, I should leave school and go to Stowe. During the Cuban missile crisis I actually packed my bag and got ready to leave the school. My classmates persuaded me to stay.

I wasn't a sports star at Miss Hall's (to say the least), but my days on the playing fields weren't as horrible as they were at Greenwich Country Day. Fall was so beautiful in the Berkshires that it mitigated my distaste for field hockey. Before our games we had to run around the hockey field, and I remember our gym teacher running after me, prodding the back of my knees with her hockey stick to encourage me to run faster.

You could get out of sports if you said you had your period, and I used this excuse so many times that after a month the school realized I was lying. In the meantime, I had a lovely time, exempt from sports, lounging on my bed, reading, and occasionally sneaking into other girls' rooms to see if they had any cookies or candy. In the winter we got to ski, but it was more trouble than it was worth. First we had to walk in our skis across several large fields to a small hill. Then we would climb up the hill and ski down it, over and over again. Once a year the whole school was bussed to Bromley, a nearby ski resort, and we had a fabulous time taking actual ski lifts up the hill.

We were allowed to go home for Thanksgiving, Christmas, and spring break, plus two weekends. Before every vacation girls would meet in the hallway and count off the days by singing:

> Ten more days 'til vacation
> Then we go to the station...
> Back to civilization...

. . . and so on. I always sang enthusiastically with the others but secretly preferred my tranquil life at boarding school to the helter-skelter at home. At home my father was so unpredictable that we never knew whether he would be Dr. Jekyll or Mr. Hyde, and mealtimes were nerve-wracking with my parents' sometimes-fraught discussions. I didn't get along with my mother and felt so inadequate around her, as I could never be as beautiful or popular. My depression certainly descended when I was at home.

Chapter Eight

One of the best things about Miss Hall's was the community of friends I made there. Since we were almost completely cut off from the outside world, we really got to know each other. We talked endlessly about boys and sex (which to many of us just meant kissing). One girl was rumored to have to gone to third base, and another was said to have gone "all the way," but that was unusual. We were all very curious about the male anatomy, and one of my friends was viewed as the expert in this area. She told us in hushed tones that our biology teacher, Mr. Provost, "sticks his penis down his left leg." I don't think Mr. Provost ever noticed us girls staring raptly at his left leg, hoping for some enlightenment.

We would also get crushes on the older girls. When I was a freshman, there was a junior who was absolutely brilliant, played the guitar, and acted flirty with the other girls. I remember her telling me that one of my dresses made me look "stacked," and my heart pounded. She went on to Radcliffe and later seemed to disappear from sight, never sending any information for class notes. My friend Prudy and I speculated wildly about what might have happened to her. A few years ago I was amazed to learn that she was the Mother Superior at a small convent in Connecticut.

One of my closest friends at Miss Hall's was Jocelyn Kress. She arrived as a "new girl" in our junior year, after going to a Swiss boarding school with prominent classmates, including Charlie Chaplin's daughters. Like me, she came from a big family—in her case, four girls and a boy. Her father, Rush, who was old

Jocelyn Kress (photo by my father)

enough to be her grandfather, had founded the Kress five-and-dime stores with his brother Sam. Together they started the Kress Collection and donated price-less Italian Renaissance paintings to museums all over the country. Jocelyn spoke perfect French and was far more chic than the rest of us. She was also drop-dead gorgeous, with classic features, wide blue eyes, and long, dark curly hair. She was supremely self-confident and given to making grand pronouncements: "Don't you know, when you go to Saks, you never pay the list price. If you bargain, you can always get it for less." I wasn't sure if this was true and would never have dared to attempt it.

When she invited me to her apartment in New York, I was gripped by anx-iety, because it would mean meeting people who presumably were far more cultivated than I was. When I entered the apartment, at 1020 Fifth Avenue, I was dazzled by the marble floors and imported palazzo ceilings, all in Italian Renaissance style. The apartment, always referred to by Jocelyn as "1020," was stunning: a twenty-room duplex penthouse overlooking Central Park and the Metropolitan Museum. There was an Antonio Moro in the foyer and a Claude Lorrain and a Rubens in the grand two-story ballroom. Other masterpieces included della Robbia sculpture and Dürer engravings, not to mention the exqui-site eighteenth-century French furniture in Mrs. Kress's bedroom.

Jocelyn entertains: "We laughed, drank champagne, and flirted like mad."

Mrs. Kress, Jocelyn's mother, was a remarkable woman and a superb hostess. There always seemed to be enough room for everyone to spend the night, and extra places were added to the table in the gorgeous French eighteenth-century dining room. When we slept over, the closets were filled with peignoirs that we could wear to breakfast. We were allowed to sleep as late as we wanted and then tell Sonja, the obliging cook, what we wanted for breakfast. And whatever the hour, someone would be sitting in the library with a bottle of Asti Spumante at the ready.

This was a big departure from my life at home. My father always insisted we appear fully dressed at breakfast at 7:30 a.m., regardless of what time we'd gone to bed the night before. (My friends who slept over after my coming-out party were horrified to learn that we were still expected in the breakfast room at the appointed hour, even though we'd all stayed up until three in the morning.) After 8:00 a.m., breakfast was no longer served, and, since the kitchen was the domain of our cook, we were not encouraged to enter.

Conversation around the Kress table was refreshingly different from my family's mealtime chitchat. The Kresses talked about art, literature, ballet, and opera. They discussed Proust and Goethe, names I was familiar with in print but had no idea how to pronounce. Prudy and I thought Goethe might be 'Goythee'. Mrs. Kress often took Jocelyn and four or five of her friends to the opera or ballet.

Our freshman year at Sarah Lawrence, we went to see an opera featuring Nicolai Ghiaurov, one of the best-known basses of the post-war period. After the performance, Mrs. Kress invited the principal singers to come back to 1020 for a party. The opera director Friedelind Wagner had a long talk with me about her family (her grandfather was Richard Wagner) and the Bayreuth Festival. Later, all the guests left except Ghiaurov, a few other friends, and me. We laughed uproariously, drank champagne, and flirted like mad. Ghiaurov was very charming to all of us, but he mainly had his eye on Jocelyn.

Mrs. Kress and her five children seemed to know everyone. Allen Ginsberg, Gregory Corso, Edie Sedgwick, Prince Alexander Romanov, and Andy Warhol all turned up at parties at 1020. Directly below the Kresses lived Prince and Princess Droutzkoy. He was a Russian émigré and she an Italian aristocrat, and they were embroiled for years in a lawsuit over her family's castle, twenty miles from the Vatican, that the Italian government had seized in the war. They had a lavish apartment filled with Russian icons and artifacts. The prince also had a huge collection of loose jewels, and once he offered me a large emerald. I was thrilled but didn't dare accept—my parents would have been horrified. Jocelyn was furious, because he had never offered one to her.

Mrs. Kress had been a ballet dancer and always had a dancer's posture. After she took us to see *Swan Lake*, she showed us some graceful swan-like movements with her arms. She was a superb ballroom dancer, and sometimes our dates would get a crush on her. She brought me into a realm of culture that I never knew even existed. She frequently took us to the Metropolitan Museum of Art to see the Kress Collection. She was also an accomplished pianist, and I could often hear her playing in the white sitting room. Jocelyn also played and made me listen to music in the recording room at Miss Hall's. She put on Dvořák's *New World Symphony* and pointed out elements I wouldn't have noticed otherwise; she also introduced me to *Romeo and Juliet* by Prokofiev. I could feel my world expanding.

As I gained self-confidence I began to make some other wonderful friends, including Prudy Painter.

Prudy was tiny, ebullient, and curvaceous, with dark hair and high cheek-bones; she looked like a young Geraldine Chaplin. Like me, she had grown up in the country. Unlike me, she was a great athlete — the captain of one of our athletic teams and a fierce competitor on the hockey field. She loved to laugh and had a contagious giggle. We spent most of our time together laughing, and we still do.

In my sophomore year, Allison Simmons, also from Greenwich, joined our class. Allison was a friend with whom I shared many adventures, including a sum-mer in Florence. She was tall, glamorous, and sophisticated. She read *The New Yorker* cover to cover each week, and she was familiar with the works of Genet, Sartre, and Carl Jung. I started reading Jung's *Memories, Dreams, Reflections* just so I could discuss it with her. I was fascinated by Jung's theory of the Collective Unconscious. According to him, the human unconscious is filled with archetypes, or universal symbols, such as the Great Mother, the Tree of Life, and many more. I tried to remember my dreams so as to observe any symbols in them.

One spring vacation during my junior year, there was no snow in Stowe, so my father decided to take the family to Israel. It was a memorable trip, not the least because we had a handsome young guide. He proudly said of his country, "Green Israel, gray Jordan," and I could really see the difference. We spent two nights in a kibbutz — one of the oldest and richest in Israel, founded in 1910. The families lived in two-floor houses, one family to each floor. There were special houses for the children and another for the babies. My mother asked one of the parents, "Don't you miss having your children at home?" The Israeli mom volleyed back: "We see our children every day and you send yours off to boarding school and don't see them for months." It was on this trip that Daddy made one of his memorable remarks; as we were wandering down some alleyway, he said: "Don't touch the walls! Men have peed on them!" My sisters and I loved repeating this remark to each other, and still do!

We went to Jerusalem, Haifa, and Caesarea, among other places. At the end of each day, as we did on every trip, we spoke into the Dictaphone about what we had seen. This was a mandatory activity and not always joyfully anticipated! Sometimes the older children would interview the younger ones. My father also spoke, and we tried to vary what we were talking about so there weren't five stories recounting the same event. After we returned home, my father's secretary would type all of it up, and my father would create a scrapbook, bound in brown leather, with photos accompanying our impressions of what we had seen.

Olive, Lucinda, and Jeannette decked out in keffiyehs

As I look back at the pictures, I notice that my hair was a burnished chestnut brown, not yet restored to its natural blond. I had thick bangs that hung like a curtain over my forehead, and if someone tried to push them away, I felt as though I were being stripped naked. The rest of my hair was in a bubble cut, which required a tyranny of rollers every night to maintain its proper effect. I also notice how well dressed all five of us girls were, always in skirts or dresses. There are amusing photos of us in keffiyehs, with only our eyes peeking through. There are also the obligatory photos of each of us on a camel. I can still say, "I see a camel," in Hebrew: "*Rakeetegamal.*"

My parents had deliberated a long time about where we should spend our summer vacations. The summer of my junior year I spent at our new home in North Haven, Maine. We summered in Greenwich until I was thirteen. When I was fourteen, we spent the first of what would be two summers at Fishers Island. I hated it, because I felt I didn't fit in, which was the way I felt about most places at that age. Most of the other kids at Fishers had been summering together from a very young age and had already formed close friendships. And like Greenwich Country Day, Fishers was all about clothes and sports. All the girls were decked out in the latest preppy fashions — McMullen blouses and shorts of every color. My wardrobe was frumpy by comparison, and I was hopeless at sports. Tennis was agony, golf a travesty, and even sailing at Fishers wasn't fun, because it was so competitive.

I can remember sitting on the beach with my father one early evening, gazing across the water at the lights along the Connecticut shoreline two miles away, and Daddy saying that he would prefer a place farther from the mainland.

When I was sixteen, we tried Camden, Maine, where my father had summered as a young teenager. Again, he felt it was too built up, and he wanted a more remote place. Nine years earlier, my parents had been shown a house in serious disrepair in nearby North Haven, a beautiful island twelve miles off the Maine coast and accessible by ferry. At the time, they thought the house was too dilapidated, but they changed their minds when my grandmother said she thought it would make a wonderful family home. As a pilot, my father was also attracted by the fact that the property, known as Oak Hill Farm, had space for an airstrip practically outside the front door. He would be able to come and go without worrying about the ferry service. Not long after we settled in, the birders in North Haven expressed concern that the planes would drive the ospreys from their nests. But the ospreys remained, and gradually the community got used to my father and his friends landing on our airstrip in a variety of planes.

My parents spent a year fixing up the place with Sister Parish, a well-known interior designer who had helped decorate the Kennedy White House. As the oldest girl, I was given first choice of bedrooms. I picked a large, comfortable room on the second floor with its own bathroom, which was a special luxury in our large household. I chose a beautiful floral pattern for the wallpaper and upholstery and could loll around happily for hours in my queendom.

We spent our first summer in North Haven when I was seventeen. I felt immediately at home. Nobody in North Haven dressed up. The more holes you had in your jeans, the cooler you were, and the holes came from wear and tear, not because the jeans were "distressed" before you bought them. After the suburban perfection of Greenwich, my mother took some time getting used to North Haven's shabby chic, but she and the rest of the family fell in love with the island and the house.

The island was inclusive, tolerant and unconcerned with social status. No one cared that I was lousy at sports, and a group of kids between the ages of thirteen and nineteen all hung out together. Unlike at Fishers, we didn't form cliques, and the girls left their McMullen blouses at home, if they had them at all. One of the boys played guitar, and we loved to sit around and sing popular songs like "Puff the Magic Dragon" or "This Land Is Your Land." That summer was a blissful haze of boat picnics, cookouts on the beach, sailing, and swimming, all set to the "surfin'" sound of a new group called the Beach Boys.

We didn't have a TV, and we certainly didn't miss it. Our house was a great attraction for our friends, because we had a heated swimming pool, a welcome respite from the frigid Maine waters. After swimming, we often played touch football on the landing strip. My sisters Susan and Helen baked brownies and brought them out after the game.

We had a large furnished barn, which was a wonderful gathering place on a rainy day. My father used to invite the whole community to come see his Charlie Chaplin movies, which we all adored. Here is Susan Minot's thinly veiled description of our property and my father from her novel *Monkeys*:

> Wilbur Kittredge had his collar turned up against his tanned skin. He was the head of a large international company...The Kittredge estate was set high on a bluff of North Eden. The main house had a long porch that overlooked the bay where humped islands scattered off into tiny dots. The estate had stables and an electric fence and guest cottages and a walled-in garden where stone satyrs huddled, ears pointed, fingers secretly at their lips. They had exotic animals [and] an American Indian had constructed authentic teepee...Each year the Kittredges had a clambake and invited the whole island—all the summer people, and certain islanders who knew who they were. But the main attraction was the carriages. Wilbur Kittredge had over forty antique carriages lined up in a special barn. There were scenes painted on the shiny doors, polished brass railings, leather seats and velvet seats and fringed surreys with wicker sides.

Daddy did have a collection of animals, old cars, and some surprising objects. We had two horses to ride around the property, and Susan and Helen each had a donkey. We had llamas (Dolly and Fernando), fainting goats (who keel over when startled because their muscles momentarily freeze), Japanese deer, an exotic breed of sheep, and reindeer.

Dolly and Fernando Llama (with our Chinese junk in the water behind them)

Every summer my father would hire someone from Brown University (we called them "the Brown Boys") to sail with us and tutor any of the children who needed help with their studies. Our first summer I had a mad crush on our "Brown Boy." In the first race I skippered, I was so distracted watching him put on his foul-weather pants that we tipped over. This was doubly ignominious, as my father was an expert sailor and the Brown Boy was captain of his sailing team.

As my mother drove me home (teeth chattering) to put on some dry clothes, I repeated my distress between sobs. When I started telling her about our tutor being captain of the Brown sailing team, my youngest sister Helen, who'd been sitting in the back seat, sobbed sympathetically and said, "And now he can't be captain anymore!"

We had a lot of fun with the islanders. The summer girls used to play basketball against the island girls, and the year-rounders always won by a huge margin. One summer we dressed up our Brown Boy as a girl, putting rollers in his hair and applying garish makeup. We all thought this was hilarious, and for once the summer girls made a respectable showing against the island girls.

Our Brown Boy that first summer felt I spent too much time in my room reading. He worked out a plan with Daylon Brown, our caretaker (Jimmy's father), to lure me out. When Daylon did the haying, he attached a lever to the back of the tractor that had to be pulled up when enough hay was gathered. I was told that Daylon needed my help pulling the lever. Years later, I realized he could have attached a string to the lever and done it himself. I enjoyed spending time with Daylon and often helped pitch the hay into his hayloft.

One day, while I was in the barn looking at his cow, I remarked to Daylon that I had always been curious about the taste of warm milk straight from the cow. According to Laura Ingalls Wilder's *Little House* books, it was delicious. Later Daylon delivered a pail of fresh milk to me. I was about to try it, but my parents said I ran a big risk of contracting a disease, and as they described the symptoms the milk looked less appealing. I was ultimately too afraid to drink it and threw it away. I returned the pail to Daylon and fibbed about how delicious the milk was.

My parents made a concerted effort to fit in with our new community. My mother looked somewhat different from the more conservative Boston ladies who summered in North Haven. She wore bright-red lipstick and perfume and loved to dress up. Chic and not shabby, she nevertheless managed to blend in.

Every July there was a big air show in Rockland, and all my father's flying buddies would come, including the writer Ernest Gann, the actor Cliff Robertson (then-married to drop-dead gorgeous Dina Merrill), and Najeeb Halaby, president of Pan Am and father of Queen Noor of Jordan. They would fly planes from the '20s, '30s, and '40s, and a lot of spectators arrived in vintage cars and period costumes. My father and Pebble Rockefeller later founded Rockland's Transportation Museum, which has a priceless collection of old planes, as well as a number of vintage cars donated by my father. One of the most beautiful is a cream-colored 1920s Rolls Royce, once owned by the silent-film star Clara Bow, which had a plush velvet interior.

Years later I learned that Pebble Rockefeller, my father's old friend, had been engaged to Margaret Wise Brown, the author of our children's favorite books (*The Runaway Bunny* and *Good Night Moon*, among others). She summered on the neighboring island of Vinalhaven. We received permission from him to go see her property, and Alex and I and Eleanor McPeck, landscape architect, reverently visited, escorted by the incomparable Foy Brown in his lobster boat. Foy is one of the owners of our local boatyard and the only person who could have navigated through the pea-soup fog that day and located the house.

When we first came to North Haven, our property didn't have many roads, so my father set out to create them. My siblings and I used to go out with him, early in the morning, in a jeep loaded with his chain saw and lots of little strips ripped from sheets. First he marked the trail he wanted with a white strip; then he cut down the trees with his chain saw, and we dragged them out of the way. Later on he let us name the paths, and we used a lot of his colorful sayings on the road signs:

"It's hard but it's fair"
"One across the mouth"
"Spare the rod and spoil the child"

And one named by Helen after our caretaker's son:

"Jimmy and his Pal Bulldozer Road"

Another of his favorite sayings—"Don't touch the walls; men have peed on them!"—we decided *not* to put on a sign.

We had horses on the property, in a big corral next to a working barn. My sisters were all better riders than I was, but we all had fun galloping around the property and practicing jumping. One day, one of my sisters and I decided to ride the horses downtown, about seven miles away. Downtown consisted of a main street with a post office, a gift shop, a grocery store called Waterman's (owned and run for many years by Franklin Waterman), and Aunt Ella's soda shop. When we arrived, we paraded our horses around (to not much attention) and then rode home.

This was a time when amphibious cars were popular. My father and several other summer people each owned one. Sometimes we'd drive across the water to Vinalhaven to see a movie. It was tremendous fun.

That first summer was, dare I say it, a pretty happy time for me. Between Miss Hall's and North Haven, I felt that I was beginning to emerge from my shell. I was comfortable with the people in both places, and so wasn't cringingly self-conscious all the time. I thought that maybe I was leaving my blues behind.

One of the most exciting things that happened at Miss Hall's was the advent of the Beatles in my senior year. I first heard them in our "Place Pigalle," a special room for seniors, where we could lounge around and listen to records. A classmate from Allentown, Pennsylvania, put on a record by this new group, and we totally flipped out. From then on, like teenage girls across the country, we were Beatles crazy. When they came to New York in February of 1964 to stay at the Plaza, we went into a frenzy. Four of us figured out a good story to get through the Plaza switchboard to the Beatles's room. For five minutes we were wild with excitement, huddled by the pay phone at Miss Hall's, feeling we were about to speak to our beloveds. Alas, we didn't get through.

The Beatles were set to appear on *The Ed Sullivan Show* on February 9, 1964, and we begged the authorities at Miss Hall's to let us watch. After much hand-wringing, they finally gave us permission. On the Big Night we all squeezed into the school's living room and sat on the floor, as close to the TV as we could get. We were admonished to keep our emotions in check: no screaming or crying. Still, when they came on, so adorable and unlike any group we had seen, we couldn't help ourselves. A few girls screamed and some of us wept.

We had endless discussions, often heated, about which Beatle was the cutest. I adored Paul and still do. The Fab Four's shaggy hairdos, derided by a lot of adults back then, would be unremarkable today. The Beatles appealed to all ages, not just to demographic groups targeted by the managers of today's rock stars. Our parents liked them, and my little sisters did. too.

I had a great teacher at Miss Hall's: Elizabeth Gatchell, later Elizabeth Klein, whose love of art was contagious. She taught us how to get the most out of museums, and we were lucky to have the Clark Art Institute fairly close by in Williamstown. Before we went to a museum, we were each presented with a pad and pencil. Miss Gatchell, or "Gatch," as she was affectionately known, told us that if we saw a painting we really liked, we should draw a sketch, in order to remember it. So many of those paintings are now imprinted on my memory. Years later, my husband and I visited "Betty" and told her we were about to visit the Clark Art Museum. Even at age ninety, she rapturously described the museum room by room, concentrating on what she felt were the best paintings.

The course I took with her my senior year was on the Italian Renaissance. This was a college-level course, and we studied the work of the leading experts on the period: Bernard Berenson, Giorgio Vasari, and many others. I got an A in the course—my only A at Miss Hall's, or anyplace else—and, forty years later, Betty still remembered the twenty-page paper I had written. I learned about the power of the Medicis, the genius of Leonardo, and the spiritual beauty of paintings, particularly those of Fra Angelico. I became fascinated with Pico della Mirandola, the fifteenth century Italian scholar and philosopher who traveled to universities in Italy and France, learning Greek, Hebrew, Syriac, and Arabic. I loved the poetry of Michelangelo and reading about the charismatic monk Savonarola and his bonfires of the vanities.

For our exam we had to draw a map of the city of Florence, highlighting all the important buildings and describing them and their contents. I was deeply impressed by the Duomo and the sculpted doors of the Baptistry. We had to memorize paintings and the artists who created them. I spent a lot of time in the library with my classmates, reviewing the paintings and quizzing one another.

I later used Gatch's method when taking my children to museums. I would always buy postcards of the major works we had seen and give a prize to the child who could identify the most paintings. This paid off when Alex and I took our two younger boys to visit an elderly friend of the family. On her desk she had a small image that our son Andrew, then eight, confidently identified: "Isn't that Leonardo da Vinci?"

The nation was convulsed my senior year, because of the assassination of President Kennedy. My mother had taken us to visit him at the White House in 1963, the spring of my junior year. I remember sitting in the Oval Office with President Kennedy. He asked my brother Tom, then at Berkshire School, why he hadn't gone to Choate. The President suggested that we children go to the East Lawn to watch Caroline ride her pony, Macaroni. Seeing us out, he came as far as the door to his office, before saying to my mother, "This is as far as I'm allowed to go." (I thought of that comment with a chill when the news came in from Dallas.)

Obligingly, we all went out to look at Caroline and her pony. She seemed oblivious to the hundreds of tourists, separated from her by a wire fence, madly snapping photos. As I came closer I was somewhat insulted to hear someone in the crowd say, "Hey, you! Get out of the way — we want Caroline."

My parents went to the White House several times for dinner, and, years later, at the exhibition of Jackie's clothes at the Metropolitan Museum, I took my mother around in a wheelchair and showed her a large blow-up of a seating chart that displayed her table at the White House.

Just before the assassination, I was sitting in the library at Miss Hall's, looking at beautiful pictures of the President, Jackie, Caroline, and John John in *Life* magazine. It seemed as though all the dreams and promises of the administration were shattered with the assassination. We watched the tragic news all day on TV, amid the weeping of both students and teachers.

I grew nostalgic during the spring of my senior year. The peaceful way of life I had enjoyed for four years was about to vanish forever. My graduation from Miss Hall's, I felt, was a truly momentous occasion. It was much more meaningful than my college graduation, which I didn't even attend. I was very excited about getting out into the real world and starting what I felt would be an extraordinary life, although I had not a clue what that would mean.

Chapter Nine

After graduating from Miss Hall's, I went home to attend a series of debutante parties, including my own. Although I didn't realize it at the time, these were some of the most beautiful parties I would ever go to. Deb parties seem a bit archaic now, but back then they were a rite of passage. "Coming out," which once meant being introduced into "society," marked the moment when girls left home and moved into the larger and freer world of college.

Lester Lanin and his band usually played at our parties. He handed out Lester Lanin hats, and we danced until the early hours. My aversion to boys had eased, to the point that I enjoyed their company and actually had fun at the parties. I went to parties in Philadelphia, Baltimore, Fishers Island, and other places, often with a group of friends and always dressed in beautiful long dresses, with white kid gloves to my elbow.

At first I didn't want to have a coming-out party of my own. As shy as I was, the prospect of being the center of attention terrified me. But my parents insisted, which was a good thing, because I ended up having a wonderful time. The boys, all well-trained by their mothers, knew that they had to dance with the debutante, so I felt like the belle of the ball.

I still have the book in which my mother planned the party, over fifty years ago, starting with the list of all the boys who were invited, some of whom I still know. As I look at the list, young faces rise up to greet me. I had a crush on "X" and invited him to be my escort, and he was late—I can still feel my old anger rise up.

My coming-out dress by Mr. Andrew of Saks

The day of the party, mother drove me into New York so that Mr. Bruno, a celebrated hairdresser, could tease my hair into a carefully sculpted bouffant creation. The expedition must have taken nearly four hours, door to door.

My dress was made by Mr. Andrew, who had his own department at Saks. It was a beautiful white-lace empire gown. In the front, lace panels opened up to show a satin underskirt. It was later remade, with black velvet in place of some of the white. I wish I still had it.

The party was held in our backyard in Greenwich, under a pink marquee with pink lining. The canopy that ran from our house to the tent was supported by poles wrapped with green-and-pink ribbons. The tables in the tent were covered with floral pink-and-peach tablecloths. We had a thirteen-piece band, led by Lester Lanin, eternally young, playing lively dance music and handing out his trademark hats. A woman dressed as Aunt Jemima—talk about politically incorrect—cooked breakfast. Some of the boys got very drunk and passed out. My parents had hired off-duty policemen who shook them awake and lined them up under the raised dance floor. The party started at 10:30 p.m. — the time I now go to bed.

After a month of coming-out parties, Jocelyn and I and her fourteen-year-old sister, Francesca, went to France to live with a French professor in a small village outside of Avignon. Although I didn't keep a diary, my friend Allison Simmons made photocopies of the long letters I wrote her and so it all comes vividly back. (Now of course I write letters infrequently and rarely receive the long, detailed letters I used to love.)

The three of us flew off to Paris, thrilled to be on our own. It was so wonderful to have some freedom: I can still remember how joyful and excited I felt. At the Paris airport, we were met by IBM people, who delivered us to a hotel that my father considered safe. We immediately left for the Café de la Paix, where I proceeded to drink four glasses of wine and suddenly found everything hysterically amusing. We were followed back to our hotel by three boys. We tried to ignore them but they kept making helpful remarks like, "Regarde la Seine." Then one would make swimming motions with his hands and say, "Glug glugglug," which seemed highly entertaining at the time.

During our time in Paris, Françoise, our sweet chaperone from IBM, kept a watchful eye on us. One day, we went to an elegant restaurant with her for lunch and then returned to our hotel to rest. We were lying down when we heard a lot of noise outside. We looked out our window and saw a large group of young people marching in the street. Francesca said, "Let's join them," which seemed like a good idea to me. We rushed out into the street, leaving Jocelyn to deal with IBM and our chaperone. We marched with the students for hours and had a great time. They were celebrating the completion of their baccalaureate. We walked down the middle of the street, enthusiastically pounding on cars and stopping traffic. It really got exciting when cars didn't stop and drove into the marchers. The group was so large that, after a while, Francesca and I couldn't have gotten out even if we had wanted to. Every once in a while the marchers would start to run, and we would be swept along. Along the way we picked up a cute French boy, who grabbed my hand whenever the crowd gathered speed; then I grabbed Francesca's, and off we went. Eventually my shoes were killing me, and I took them off to go barefoot. I still remember this as one of the most exhilarating afternoons I've ever had.

We arrived back at our hotel to find Françoise anxiously waiting for us. At dinner we wore beautiful dresses, bought just that morning, along with incredibly sexy French underwear (pale blue satin with an overlay of black lace). Jocelyn and I spent most of our summer budget on these purchases. Later, we couldn't afford to rent bikes and had to hitch rides with other students.

Françoise had come up with dates for Jocelyn and me. Mine was a quite handsome and sophisticated twenty-four-year-old. Jocelyn's was not at all appealing, and I remember her whispering in my ear in the back of the limousine, "Goddamn IBM." The next day we drove to Versailles, where Mr. Van der Kemp, the curator, took us on a special tour. Jocelyn's family, the Kresses, were good friends of the Van der Kemps, and the Kress Foundation had given generously to the restoration of Versailles. Jocelyn told me that, while she was growing up in Arizona, her family was still holding some of Marie Antoinette's furniture, and, in fact, Marie Antoinette's bedspread was stored under Jocelyn's bed! I wasn't feeling well, so I rested in one of the Van der Kemps's beds. Because Mr. Van der Kemp's apartment was part of the estate, I am able to say that I slept at Versailles, which may account for my fascination with Marie Antoinette. Here's an excerpt from a letter I wrote a friend:

> The French think the Americans are infants, rich uncivilized brutes who trample over everyone else and who have never suffered because we haven't had a foreign war that affected us. They also resent me because I represent IBM—hence all the American Companies that are taking over France and forcing French Companies out of business like Libby's canned food which is climbing its way to the top. I'm sick of hearing about barbarian Americans—business men in particular.

Jocelyn, Francesca, and I traveled by train to Avignon, where we were picked up by Madame and Monsieur D'Anselme. Madame D'Anselme ran a summer school out of her home, which was an old farmhouse. The third floor had bedrooms for boarders. Jocelyn and I bunked together and shared the floor—and one bathroom—with three other girls. In the mornings we studied—all at different levels. Jocelyn, having been to boarding school in Switzerland, spoke excellent French, while I was much less proficient. I remember reading *Le Grand Meaulnes*, which enthralled me. We were free after lunch to relax, do homework, or go to a nearby swimming hole, where we competed for the attentions of a sexy, swarthy, black-bikini-clad fellow named Bernard, who rode his motorcycle there every afternoon. My triumph of the summer was when he told me I looked the best of our group in a bikini. It was the first time I had worn one.

I got in trouble with our hosts after I inadvertently introduced a drug dealer into the household. A friend of mine sent a bearded young man to our village, describing him as "a Danish count." Always a sucker for royalty, I agreed to go out with him a few times. Luckily I left France soon after meeting him, but he went on to date one of the other girls at the house (a student at Sarah Lawrence who used to count her sleeping pills every night to make sure she had a sufficient number to kill herself). The "Danish count"—in reality, a Danish cook—was arrested for drug dealing, and the police questioned the D'Anselmes. It was written up in the newspapers, marking a minor setback for Franco-American relations. This is an excerpt from a letter Mme. D'Anselme sent my father:

> Our girls are, rightly so, protected at home and perhaps do not have enough 'sixth sense' to feel that a person is definitely not their own kind. Both my husband and I had met this boy <u>once</u> and had a difficult time persuading the girls he was a freak and a fraud and at best a strange sort of guy, although this was quite evident to us on first meeting. We forbade all the girls to see him, refused to have him in the house and allowed Jeannette to go <u>outside</u> to talk to him for a few minutes <u>only</u> one afternoon, in order to tell him none of our girls would see him. When several of them met him at a café that same evening, it was without our knowledge. As you probably know, we do allow the girls to invite their friends in the house and welcome them for dinner...The very fact we didn't offer anything like this to the boy in question had a very obvious meaning.
>
> I didn't mean to 'lecture' about this, but I wanted you to know our point of view and to clear any misunderstanding that might have occurred through knowing about this from other persons. This is the only time something like this has occurred in many summers, and I am sure it was an unfortunate 'concours de circonstances,' not to occur ever again.

〜

In the fall I started at Sarah Lawrence College, which I chose because, along with Bennington, it had the fewest rules. Sarah Lawrence is in Bronxville, only a half hour from Manhattan. I remember being totally intimidated by my classmates. They seemed to "be" something already. One girl was the daughter of Paul Draper, the noted tap dancer and choreographer, and she was a professional dancer herself. The pop singer Lesley Gore was in our class and already famous for "It's My Party" and "Judy's Turn to Cry." Our class president, Jane Stanton, had written several plays and knew Truman Capote and other celebrities. One of our most notable alumna was Hope Cooke, the Queen of Sikkim (which is now part of India). She later became a friend.

It was comforting to have Jocelyn with me at college. We were placed next door to each other, paired with two girls who had gone to Farmington (another all-girls boarding school), Margaret Turnbull and Sandy Schoelkopf. We all became great friends and hung out together, mainly at the Kresses'. After going out on dates in the city, we often met at Grand Central Station to take the last train back to Bronxville, so we could get back before curfew. We were housed in ugly modern glass dorms. I didn't find the campus or the hodgepodge of buildings appealing, though in the spring there was a lovely archway covered in an explosion of wisteria.

I felt totally overwhelmed, inadequate, and paralyzed by social anxiety. My depression, which had lifted at Miss Hall's and North Haven, returned in full force.

My first year, I lost weight because I couldn't face going to the dining room by myself and joining a group of strangers. The food in the dining room was inedible—as bad as the food at Greenwich Country Day. Whenever I could, I'd go to the "caf" and get a hamburger. I didn't do this often, because most of my fifty-dollars-a-month allowance was spent on train rides into the city, taxis, movies, and even some clothes.

Our classes were small and demanded a lot of student participation. These discussions were a source of agony, because I lacked the self-confidence to express myself. The girls didn't seem friendly, but I'm sure this was due in part to my own reticence. Today I could happily sit in class and pontificate.

When I was a freshman, my father wrote a letter in triplicate to his three oldest daughters:

Dear <u>Jeannette</u>, Olive and Lucinda, [Jeannette was underlined.]

I am sitting alone in my office having sent my secretary home. I have been thinking about boys. I know quite a bit about them as I used to be one myself.

One thing about boys is they are always looking for new frontiers. They will try to cross the widest river, or scale the highest mountain. Often when they have accomplished their goal they will move on to something else.

It is the same thing with girls and if the boys find they get what they want too easily they will often move on to the next.

I care about all of you and want you to have happy experiences.

With love,
Daddy

In retrospect, I can see that this was a sweet letter with a good measure of truth in it, and I wish I had been more appreciative at the time. Instead I thought it was absolutely hilarious and entertained my dorm mates by reading it aloud.

Sarah Lawrence didn't have much campus life, because many of the girls went to their homes in the city on weekends. My parents felt I should be bonding with my fellow students, but it was difficult to do any bonding with so few girls around. This wasn't a problem during my freshman and sophomore years, because I spent most weekends at Jocelyn's apartment. From there I would go out on dates, usually with boys I'd met at coming-out parties or sons of my parents' friends. The best part of the weekends was arriving back at 1020 and sitting up at until all hours with Jocelyn and our friends—gossiping, watching old movies, and eating her cook Senya's great chocolate chip cookies.

The fall of my freshman year, I flew to Washington to watch President Johnson present my father with the Presidential Medal of Freedom. It was very exciting to be back at the White House. I can still remember Ladybird's warmth when she greeted us: "So nice of ya'll to come down." The other recipients included Aaron Copland, Walt Disney, Helen Keller, Edward R. Murrow and Lynn Fontanne. My father was like a stage-struck schoolboy with Fontanne and her husband Alfred Lunt, two actors he admired enormously. We saw them having breakfast at the same coffee shop in our hotel before the ceremony.

During spring vacation of my freshman year, my father took all five of his girls to Japan. My brother was in the army in Korea and able to get a six-day leave to spend time with us.

On the plane over, all five girls stretched out on the floor. The steward said it was against regulations; my father disagreed; and soon the conversation became so heated that the steward fetched the regulation book and triumphantly read the rules outloud to Daddy. (We were flying tourist class, as was usual for us, as Daddy could be frugal. Sometimes my parents did fly first class while we children traveled in tourist.) The flight seemed endlessly long, with a one-hour stopover in Chicago, followed by ten hours to Tokyo.

After lunch on our first day in Tokyo, Daddy announced that he would buy us all kimonos. We went to a department store, where he left us with a saleslady in the kimono department while he went to the camera department. My kimono was gorgeous: pale lavender with light-pink flowers. We picked out obis and other strings with which to tie the kimonos. The outfits were completed with special shoes and socks. When my father returned, he was horrified at the bill but gamely paid it. It took us an hour to put on our kimonos when we posed for the picture on the family Christmas card.

In Nikko, we were fascinated by the Japanese farmhouse where we were staying. On the first floor were two cows lying on straw. The family lived on the second and third floors. My youngest sisters were amazed and giggled when our hosts actually got down on the floor to respectfully bow to us. We slept on Japanese beds, more like mats on the floor with Japanese covers. The meals were very different from what we were used to, with a lot of raw fish, which my father liked, but that none of the rest of us could eat.

During the trip, my sisters and I always addressed our father as Honorable Father and ourselves as Number One or Two or Three (whichever we were) Sister, or Honorable Sister.

We were always extremely well dressed—no slacks or sneakers. In pictures from this trip, I notice my hair looking slightly more becoming. The bangs weren't so thick and the hair was the same length everywhere else—no more bubble cut. My father's photos were getting more and more artistic, with wonderful street scenes and landscapes. At one of our dinners we were seated on the traditional

Dressed like natives in our new kimonos

tatami mats, while a geisha with traditional white face paint and an elaborate hairdo performed for us. We visited many pagodas and temples and fed the tame deer at Nara. We even travelled by boat on the Inland Sea.

I am touched to notice that, at the end of the trip, my father composed a poem for each of us. Here is mine:

> The girl who knows more about reading
> Than Mother or Dad or us all
> Brilliant and modest — retiring
> Makes us parents feel twenty feet tall!
>
> Kidding her as a bookworm
> Saying she's always in books
> Now tables are turning
> She's the envy of even the cooks!
>
> She seems to know where she's going
> Know what she wants to be
> Remembering trip from Bermuda
> It certainly won't be to sea!

I wanted to work in New York City in the summer after my freshman year. My uncle Peter was involved with the Salvation Army, and his friend Major Gladys Goddard got me a job caring for three-year-olds at a day care center in Brooklyn. I thought it would be fun to have my own apartment, but my parents gave me a choice: I could either live with my aunt for the summer, in her beautiful, large, well-staffed apartment, or I could stay in a tiny room at the Barbizon (at that time a residential hotel for women only) and pay for it myself, out of my meager salary. Needless to say, I took the free lodgings at my aunt's. I learned how to navigate the subway and enjoyed being with the children, despite no air-conditioning at the center and feeling exhausted at the end of the day.

I slipped back into the dark shadows of depression during my sophomore year and spent much of my time sleeping. At this point my friends were all absorbed with their own lives and beginning to have their own first love affairs. Somehow it seemed to open a crevasse between us: as though they were suddenly grown up and I remained an immature child. It was the same routine every day: wake up feeling unbearably sad—go to class—lunch—sleep—dinner—study—and try to find someone to type my papers. Many of us had arrived at college not knowing how to type, and I spent a lot of my allowance on typing services.

We had some wonderful teachers, Bill Rubin and Joseph Campbell among them. However, students had to audition for these classes, and it was rumored that the two professors only took the most beautiful girls. Students would go to their interviews dressed provocatively in their shortest skirts, with lots of makeup and lavish sprays of perfume. I was afraid to even try. I did audit some of Bill Rubin's lectures, which were among the most brilliant I heard at Sarah Lawrence. I wish I had attended every one. I was so lucky to be surrounded by so many smart people, but I didn't appreciate it at the time. So many girls flourished in this intellectual atmosphere, and the teachers were great mentors.

I met Jackie Bograd at Sarah Lawrence, and we became great friends years later, when we both moved back to New York City. Jackie is Latin, pretty, petite, and vivacious, the oldest of four sisters. She was a brilliant student of all the great teachers: Ada Bozeman, Joseph Campbell, and Barbara Rose. Her artwork was fabulous and still looks great many years later.

Another bright spot was Bill Park's class in eighteenth-century English literature. I fell in love with English country houses surrounded by gardens designed by Capability Brown. I envied the rarefied world of travel, theater, letter writing, and grand parties on Belgrave Square. Boswell's *London Journal* captivated me, with its descriptive powers and critical self-examination. I went on to read *The Complete Journals* with the same devotion. *Clarissa* by Richardson was another favorite, along with *Pride and Prejudice* and, of course, *Tom Jones*. I became somewhat politically conscious at this time and took part in a protest march against the Lawrence Hospital in Bronxville. The aides and other workers (mainly black) were being grossly underpaid. We all sang "We Shall Overcome."

In my junior year, I was pursued by a young law student named Ralph McElvenny. I met him at my cousin Walker Buckner's wedding. I was considering going out with him, and my suitemate, my old friend Siri Larsen, encouraged me. "Yes, you should go," she said. "He's very handsome." He was intelligent and had a good sense of humor. I was extremely lonely and, as usual, somewhat depressed. I reveled in his attention and having company on weekends. I have often thought that, if Jocelyn had not been in Paris, my life might have taken a different turn. I confessed my feelings to her in a letter dated January 30, 1966: "I wrote you about Ralph last November and I guess that was when I started to realize this was different from anything." To be honest, this is when I started sleeping with him. (Until then, I had counted myself the oldest virgin at Sarah Lawrence. Wearing a girdle had turned out to be like a kind of chastity belt, as by the time some ardent boy started pulling it off—an arduous process—the spell had been broken and I had changed my mind. Of course my virginity, such as it was at that point, was kind of a technicality.) I had never loved anyone so completely before, and the only thing I worried about was whether my parents would let me get married that June.

My parents, as it happened, were not pleased. They felt I was too young—and, as it turned out, they were right. I was only twenty-one (Ralph was twenty-five), but it was a still a time when young women hoped for "a ring by spring" of their senior year. I jumped the gun by a year, which must seem crazy to women today who postpone marriage until their thirties. My engagement came before "women's lib" revolutionized gender roles, and Ralph and I were never on anything close to equal footing. My alarm bells should have gone off when he began monitoring my weight even before we were married. As I wrote in a letter at the time, "Ralph has got me on this physical fitness kick—no fattening food—lots of running and exercise every night." When we'd go out and I'd order French fries,

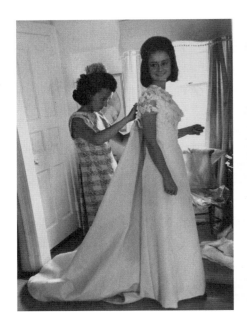

LEFT: Mummy pins on my train (photo by Toni Frissell)

RIGHT: The bride, only twenty-one, on her wedding day (photo by Toni Frissell)

he'd say, "Do you really need that?" But he was persistent, he was smart, and he seemed interested in what I had to say. And he made me laugh, no small thing to someone who felt gloomy so much of the time.

The wedding that June was large, with about 350 people attending. Again a huge tent was erected on our Greenwich property, this one blue with pink lining. The tablecloths and slipcovers for the chairs were a paler blue. The bridesmaids wore pink—my favorite color. My parents' friend, the eminent photographer Toni Frissell, gave me a beautiful gift of wedding photos she took. (She also documented the family at various other events.) Despite all this, I felt like a minor participant. My friends were greatly outnumbered by business leaders and prominent politicians who were friends of my parents but had little or no connection to me.

Once again, Mr. Andrew from Saks created my dress. He incorporated a Victorian lace collar and veil originally made for my mother's grandmother by nuns in Brussels. The high neck flowed into an off-white (the same color as the ancient veil and collar) columnar dress with a satin skirt that widened toward the ankles. Attached to my shoulder was a train that trailed after me. (Mr. Andrew's

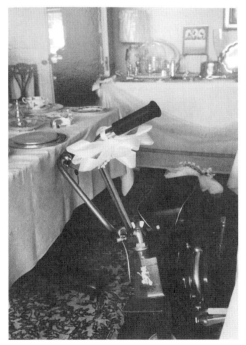

TOP: The "loot" (photo by Toni Frissell)

BOTTOM: Larry's motorcycle (photo by Toni Frissell)

creation was so unlike the beautiful strapless dresses the young women wear now. In the mid '60s brides were still covered up and delivered — theoretically, at least — as virginal presents to their husbands). The Victorian lace collar turned out to be very unlucky — most of the brides in our family who wore it got divorced.

For a few days before and during the wedding, all our gifts were put on display in my parents' dining room. I was excited when the gifts started coming in, and looked forward to opening them. Alas, my mother, afraid I would not keep a proper record, had hired a social secretary for this purpose; after opening each gift, the secretary entered the item, and the name and address of the giver, in a special book. When I look at photos of the gifts now, I realize I could have opened a small store and done a brisk business selling the china, glass, and silver that we had registered for at Tiffany & Co. The gift that was the most fun was a small motorcycle from Larry Rockefeller.

My heart belongs to Daddy (photo by Toni Frissell)

Chapter Ten

In my senior year, I commuted to college from Manhattan. I was majoring in early childhood education, which I found fascinating. I was also busy taking care of our apartment on East Eighty-Sixth Street and cooking our meals: woman's work! I had to write over 300 thank-you notes for our wedding gifts. I was in the early stages of pregnancy and not feeling well, which was why I didn't attend my own graduation.

In mid-June, my husband and I packed up and flew to San Francisco, where Ralph had lined up a job. We settled at 1170 Sacramento, a high-rise apartment on Nob Hill, overlooking Grace Cathedral and Huntington Park. It was a spectacular location, but an unusual spot for a young couple. Most of our contemporaries lived on the outskirts of the city, in houses with yards.

By this time, I had very little contact with my parents. I was determined to be independent and to put my unhappiness behind me. Every morning, Ralph would go off to work, and I would be home alone. I had joined the Junior League, because my mother said it would help me meet people when I moved to a new city. I called the League and was told that it was inactive during the summer. After that, I couldn't think of other ways to meet people. As unhappy as I had been growing up, I had never lacked for companionship. I had my sisters at home, and I was surrounded by girls my age at Miss Hall's and Sarah Lawrence. Now I was plain lonely. As much as I loved to read, I longed for friends and conversation. Many days the only person I spoke to was the butcher when I picked up meat for dinner.

One evening, when Ralph and I went to a party with other couples, I met another young pregnant woman, and we struck up a conversation. I confided to her how lonely I was, and she gave me her phone number, urging me to call. I hung onto the precious piece of paper with the number on it. After several days I screwed up my courage and called her. I introduced myself and a long silence followed. She had forgotten who I was. I quickly and clumsily got off the phone, devastated and discouraged. My first friend was an elderly woman who lived in the building, a Mrs. Black, the mother-in-law of Shirley Temple Black. We used to go across the street for butterscotch sundaes.

In time, Ralph and I met some nice couples and made friends. I also occupied myself reading about the history of the city and the arduous westward trek of the pioneers in the Donner Party, some of whom turned to cannibalism to survive. I particularly enjoyed Irving Stone's *Men to Match My Mountains*, a fascinating collection of stories about the settling of Utah, Colorado, and California.

When our son Ralph Watson McElvenny arrived, I was ecstatic and thought I had the most exquisite baby in the history of the universe. But my manic ecstasy soon changed to depression. After baby Ralph was born, I felt extremely tired, and so husband Ralph would go out to dinner with our friends while I stayed at home in bed. It was all I could do to drag myself out of bed every morning with an incredible weight of sadness bearing down on me. Nothing at that point gave me any pleasure, even my beautiful baby. I had no interest in anything—current events, friends, even my beloved books failed to capture me. I woke in the morning not knowing how I would be able to get through the day. I felt that I was worse than nothing, surrounded by a heavy layer of grief and sadness. It was always a relief when the evening approached and I knew there was not a lot of time left until I could have the relief of oblivion in my sleep. Before long I had a complete breakdown and could not stop crying. My husband attempted to cheer me up by taking me out to lunch. Sitting at Blum's, across the street from our apartment, the noises in the restaurant kept getting louder and louder in my head until I ran out of the restaurant with my hands over my ears.

My gynecologist kindly came to our apartment, and, between sobs, I poured out my heart to him. I said I was terrified to be alone with my baby and worried I might throw us both out the window. I had heard a radio report when I was at Sarah Lawrence about the wife of an African diplomat who had done just that. The story haunted me, because she had lived in the same building on Eighty-Sixth

Street as Ralph and I did. I later learned that she didn't speak English, had no friends in her new community, and was suffering from isolation. I can remember clutching baby Ralph and saying resolutely to myself, I won't throw *this* baby out the window (as though it was fine to throw any other baby out!).

Things had also changed with my husband. Instead of taking me seriously, as he seemed to do before we were married, he no longer seemed charmed by my opinions. We seemed to have nothing in common, and even on our weekends we were mostly apart, he at the golf course and I with our son.

Unable to cope, I checked into the hospital for the first of two treatments for postpartum depression. The first time, I stayed in a hospital across the street from where we lived. I was relieved to be in a place where I couldn't harm my baby or myself. I had electroshock treatments (now known as electroconvulsive therapy) that alleviated my depression fairly quickly. I cannot remember these treatments, except sleeping all day afterwards, which was a huge relief from the miserable life I had been living. The only problem was that, when I was released and went home, I had lost my memory of recent events. People would call, and I would have to say, "I'm sorry, I don't remember you. I just had shock treatment." That was quite a conversation stopper!

The treatment became viewed as barbaric, but milder shock therapy is now making a comeback and can be very helpful for someone suffering from deep depression. How it works is still somewhat of a mystery. A recent study found that the induced seizures disrupt the normal pattern of blood flow to the left side of the brain, which is associated with negative thoughts and anxiety. Uplifting, optimistic emotions are more commonly associated with the right hemisphere.

After the treatments I was level for a while, then I'd go into a manic phase that was quite fun. I should have had follow-up counseling to figure out why I had become so depressed in the first place, and also to support me for the next several months. Instead I gave a big party, only to feel depression start to envelope me again. Then I decided to take tennis lessons, but my lack of ability made me sink even lower. This time my husband took me to Michigan, hoping his parents could help me get the treatment that I needed.

I stayed in a hospital called Mercywood Sanitarium in Ann Arbor, not far from where my in-laws lived in Grosse Pointe. Run by the Sisters of Mercy, it was a private mental institution on eighty acres, with gardens, tennis courts, and a bowling alley—none of which I used. It opened in 1924 and was torn down after it

The mental hospital where I had a second round of electroshock treatments

closed in 1986. Looking at an old photo of Mercywood, I am reminded of a creepy place in an Alfred Hitchcock movie.

When I arrived, I was put on an upper floor with the most disturbed (but not dangerous) people. I was fascinated, despite my depression, to observe the behavior of the other patients. One woman rocked frenetically in her rocking chair. Others had quite animated conversations with themselves.

Fairly soon, I was moved to a lower floor, where my "treatment" mainly consisted of more electric shock. I would be brought in quite early and given an anesthetic, electrodes would be attached to my temples for the administration of the "shock," and then I'd sleep for the rest of the day. Beyond this, I have no recollection of what I did. I can't remember if I ate in my room or in the dining room. I did have a roommate, but retain no memory of her. I was relieved to be there, as I felt I was "safe" and would not be hurting myself or my baby. At this point, my wonderful mother-in-law, Betsy McElvenny, was taking care of baby Ralph. Between treatments, I was given a lot of medication. I recently discussed this period with my sister Susan, who said she and my parents came to visit. She told me I looked sad and slightly unkempt. I have no recollection of seeing them there.

I was released after about six weeks, and my husband and I settled in Grosse Point. Ralph had found a new job, and we moved into a large brick house on

Ralphie and Edith in Grosse Pointe (photo by me)

Ridge Road with our baby and a daily maid (now I would say "housekeeper") named Edith, who wore a white uniform. When we first bought the house, the grass had not been cut for some time, and the lawn was a riot of daisies and dandelions. I thought they looked pretty and wanted to leave the lawn in its natural state. But soon I got calls from my neighbors asking me to cut the lawn, so that it resembled their own well-manicured ones, which I reluctantly did.

I had always hated the suburbs, but there I was, in a place even more insular than Greenwich, Connecticut.

I adored my in-laws: They were great parent surrogates and treated me like a daughter. When Ralph went on a business trip, his mother Betsy would come over to pick up baby Ralph and me and bring us back to her house. Assisted by Ruth, her longtime housekeeper, Betsy cooked dinner every night, and she, my father-in-law, and I ate by candlelight. Betsy adored Dean Martin and we always watched his show, which I enjoyed too. Mr. and Mrs. McElvenny Sr. were devoted to each other, and it was lovely being in such a harmonious atmosphere. Betsy had a wonderful sense of humor, and we often giggled together.

Gradually I became involved with the community through the Junior League. I started doing volunteer work on Friday afternoons and, ironically enough, I did counseling for Planned Parenthood—little knowing that my next husband,

Alexander, a grandson of Margaret Sanger (founder of the group that became Planned Parenthood), would become the president of Planned Parenthood of New York City.

My father-in-law, Ralph T. McElvenny, was president of the American Natural Gas Company and a prominent member of the Detroit business community, as well as a central figure in the Detroit renaissance. He invited Minoru Yamasaki, who would go on to become the lead architect of the World Trade Center in Manhattan, to design a high-rise building for his company in the heart of Detroit's civic center on Woodward Avenue. The building was set on a pedestal and surrounded by gardens. I can remember visiting it and enjoying the decorative façade and impressive lobby. Giacomo Manzu created an eleven-foot-high bronze sculpture of a ballet dancer, modeled on his wife, that stood in a fountain outside the building.

Mr. McElvenny once rescued me from jail. I was driving into Detroit to go to the dentist and was pulled over for not putting on my signal light when I turned. I was horrified to be stopped by a police car with two officers. When they asked for my license, I didn't have it. Then they asked for my registration, and I didn't have that either. I cried and begged to be let off, promising never to do it again, but they took me to the police station and locked me up with women who looked like hookers. (Of course now everybody looks like a hooker, as there is not much difference in dress.) I was allowed one phone call and I used it to reach Mr. McElvenny. He came over immediately, and said to the police officers, "After the big contribution we gave you, *this* is the way you treat my daughter?" We swept out of there with great dignity, and later on, when the court date came up, my case miraculously disappeared.

I made a few local friends, including Bicky Kellner and her sister Kathy. However, the closest friend was Jody Zara. We took a ballet exercise class together a few mornings a week and would often have coffee afterwards. One week I read about a course in witchcraft that was being given at a local community center. Jody and I were eager to try it. We joked about the dress code and decided that the class uniform should definitely be black.

Gundella, our teacher, said she was descended from a long line of witches. The class helped us develop our intuitive powers through various exercises. In one instance, I was paired with a man I had never seen before. Holding a pendulum, I asked him a series of yes or no questions. I would predict his answers according to

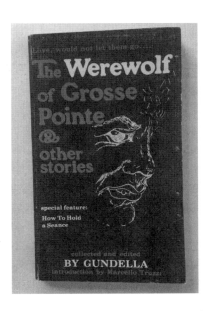

Some tips from my witchcraft teacher in Michigan

whether the pendulum went up and down (yes) or sideways (no). My predictions were uncannily accurate. We also did experiments with plants, including playing music to them. I found it all fascinating but wasn't ready to enter the realm of intuition. The power of thoughts frightened me, because I was having dreams that were disturbing. I recently found a book by Gundella in my Maine library called *The Werewolf of Grosse Pointe*.

At the same time I was taking the Witchcraft Course, Jody and I were exploring other realms with her Ouija board. We always did it at Jody's house, and I still remember the bizarre feeling when the planchette started pulling our fingers around the board, spelling out words which neither of us had control over. Eventually we were in contact with a spirit called Ann who had been executed as a witch in the thirteenth century. She asked us to pray for her. After about a fifteen- or twenty-minute "conversation," I would be exhausted and often had a terrible head ache. Years later, when I sold James Merrill's *Book of Ephraim*, about his Ouija board experiences, at my bookstore, I felt my own Ouija board exploration became more elevated and poetic. Here are Jody's recollections:

Ann was a 16th c. woman, named a witch and burned at the stake for having murdered a child during one of her rituals. As I remember she admitted she was guilty of it. -She was burning in Hell for her sins and approached us to get her a Plenary Indulgence from the Catholic Church so she could be transferred to Heaven.

The Catholic Church's Plenary Indulgence was a specific prayer said by loved ones on earth that had the power to release a soul from Purgatory and send it on to Heaven. The practice by priests of selling these at a very steep price to their faithful was one of the great scandals of the Catholic Church, and one which gave fuel to the fire of the Reformation.

Ann's request was impossible to fulfill because in the Catholic Church's doctrine Hell is a No Exit kind of place.

Ann was so furious when we told her our hands were tied she began swearing at us, using most colorful and vulgar language. This, of course, was definitive proof that neither of us was influencing the Ouija board, because we didn't even know those words ;). She would break into later sessions and randomly swear at us before departing again.

After I told a friend about our Ouija experience with Ann she asked to borrow my board. Several days later she returned it saying it was demonically possessed. At the time I was teaching at the Medical School at Wayne State U. A Father Markowicz had his office next to mine and over time we became good friends. When I shared with him a little of our Ouija board's story he said I should destroy it. In the end I gave it to him and he burned it.

Among the people we knew, conversations often seemed to be about how much someone's house cost or what family they were from—the automobile Fords, or the chemical Fords? I was treated kindly, but except for Jody and a few others, I didn't really connect with people in Grosse Pointe. I entertained myself by reading fairly light historical novels by Gwen Bristow, starting with *Jubilee*

Trail, an adventure story about two women in the mid-nineteenth century who traveled out west.

I am now reading *Main Street* by Sinclair Lewis, and these passages reminded me so much of my Grosse Pointe life:

> She listened to the Smails and Kennicott trying to determine by dialectics whether the copy of the Dauntless, which Aunt Bessie wanted to send to her sister in Alberta, ought to have two or four cents postage on it. Carol would have taken it to the drug store and weighed it, but then she was a dreamer, while they were practical people (as they frequently admitted). So they sought to evolve the postal rate from their inner consciousnesses, which, combined with entire frankness in thinking aloud, was their method of settling all problems.

> A village is a force seeking to conquer the earth...Sure of itself, it bullies other civilizations, as a traveling salesman in a brown derby conquers the wisdom of China and tacks advertisements of cigarettes over arches for centuries dedicated to the sayings of Confucius. Such a society functions admirably in the production of cheap automobiles, dollar watches, and safety razors. But it is not satisfied until the entire world also admits that the end and joyous purpose of living is to ride in flivvers, to make advertising-pictures of dollar watches, and in the twilight to sit talking and not of love and courage but of the convenience of safety razors.

I turned to food for comfort, as I used to do when I was a young girl, and became the heaviest I have ever been. I was addicted to Sara Lee Brownies, and when Ralph was away I'd get up late, put my baby in the car seat, drive to the 7-Eleven to pick up the brownies, and devour the whole package with a glass of milk. The next morning I'd have a sugar hangover and feel ashamed of my body. My matronly life made me feel so much older than I was—older, in fact, than I feel now. On my twenty-fifth birthday, Ralph said to me, "Just think—you are a quarter of a century old." It seemed more like a full century to me.

We socialized with about four other couples and would hold elaborate dinners for each other. I relied on Julia Child's cookbook, spending hours on

Portrait with pearls shortly after my move to New York City

a chicken recipe that I wouldn't dream of cooking now. For dessert I impressed everyone with my crêpes suzette.

In looking at photos of myself at the time, I notice that the unhappier I was, the more I teased my hair. I would not have looked out of place at the French court of Louis XVI.

When Ralphie was around two, I became pregnant again. One evening, when I was nearly three months along, I began spotting, and later that night, I lost the baby. I didn't want to wake up my husband, but in the morning, I asked to be driven to the hospital. As I was having an emergency D&C, the doctor cheerfully said, "You know what we call this?" (Pause, chuckles.) "*Love's Labour's Lost.*" Even though I always enjoyed a good laugh, I didn't find the remark at all funny. Losing the baby was a metaphor for my life. I was dying inside in Grosse Pointe.

To survive, I created a parallel fantasy life in which I lived in Manhattan. I loved reading Suzy's column in the *New York Post* about the glamorous people there. I avidly followed the social perambulations of Pat Buckley, Nan Kempner, and others. I wanted to know them and go to the same fabulous parties and wear couture clothes. I also devoured Liz Smith's gossip column in the New York *Daily News*. Along with the society columns, I read books by Gloria Steinem and Betty Friedan, and Erica Jong's *Fear of Flying* made a huge impression on me.

Because I had married so young, I had missed out on the freedoms that women were enjoying for the first time — social, economic, and sexual. I had dated relatively little, had rarely worked outside the home, and had slept with only one man. I felt that life was passing me by. I wanted to be part of the exciting world of New York City.

Chapter Eleven

After three years in Grosse Pointe, Ralph got a job offer in New York, and I encouraged him to take it. Needless to say, I was ecstatic about going to the city of my dreams. We moved to an apartment on the Upper East Side, and I started to reconnect with old friends.

Shortly after our move, my friend Prudy Painter invited me to be a bridesmaid in her wedding to a handsome young man from Germany. Ralph and I drove to her parents' home in Norfolk, Connecticut, for the ceremony.

It was a perfect fall weekend, and at the reception, one of the ushers, another charming young German, asked me to dance. He waltzed beautifully, and I started enjoying myself. He kept cutting in, and I was flattered by his attentions. After the wedding I went back to married life, but the usher called me to invite me out, and I began to wonder if the single life might be fun. As my confidence grew, I began thinking more and more about the possibility of divorce. I felt divorce was a big stigma. No one in my family had been divorced, and I puritanically felt I should keep my wedding vows. In my fragile state, I saw it as a choice between ending my marriage or resigning myself to a lifetime of unhappiness. At one point I felt my mind idly wondering if there were any painless non-detectable poison I might slip into my husband's coffee and thus have the glory of widowhood without the taint of divorce. In Agatha Christie novels this seemed to happen quite easily...would there be a Hercule Poirot to find me out? I was quite horrified by my thought and realized divorce was my only option.

One night I lay awake on the chaise in our bedroom watching my husband sleep. The minute he woke up, I simply said, "I want a divorce." My mother-in-law wept when I told her. "Betsy, you see how unhappy I am, you know I can't stay," I said. "I know, but don't leave," she replied. "I don't want you to go."

Within a few weeks of my decision, young Ralph and I moved out of the apartment, eventually ending up at Seven Gracie Square, where I lived for the next forty years.

I had gone directly from my parents' house to my husband's, and now, at twenty-five, I was on my own for the first time. I reveled in my new freedom. I felt like the ex-wife in the Woody Allen movie *Play It Again, Sam* — like her, I wanted to laugh, and I wanted to ski. I wanted to ski down the hill laughing like a maniac. I had plenty of time for myself, but at first I wasn't sure what to do with it. I explored the city again, often wandering around by myself late at night with a sense of pure exhilaration.

I renewed old friendships, and made some wonderful new ones, including Pam Loxton and Clara Dale, whom I met when Ralph joined the toddlers at Central Presbyterian Nursery School on Park Avenue and Sixty-Fourth Street. I also reconnected with Bicky Kellner, whose son Peter was Ralph's age.

My friends took me to the Yves St. Laurent store on Madison Avenue. How we loved the silk blouses with bows that tied around our necks. The peasant blouses and skirts were other favorites. I adored the dramatic, flattering designs. My friend Jackie Bograd and I often shopped together, even buying identical outfits. Once we were happily walking down Madison Avenue in our matching Sonia Rykiel ensembles, complete with a pinned-on artificial flower; we thought we looked great, but a friend approaching us on the sidewalk couldn't stop laughing.

We went to lunch at the fabulous restaurants that dotted the Upper East Side. At the top of the list was Gino's, on Lexington near Sixty-First. We'd order pasta with the *segreto* sauce and think nothing of downing several glasses of wine before staggering up Madison Avenue and making some ill-advised purchases. One of our old haunts, Le Veau d'Or, is still on Sixtieth, between Lexington and Park, but many others have disappeared. I especially miss Madame Romaine's, then at 133 East Fifty-Sixth Street, which was known for its wonderful omelets. Swifty's, another favorite, recently closed its doors.

Around this time, my friends and I started reading Edith Wharton. We identified with Lily Bart in *The House of Mirth*, and kept hoping she would have a different and happier life. As I reread it and saw all the poor choices she made, I silently spoke to Lily, imploring her not to flout convention, even though I understood her motives.

I loved the Metropolitan Museum and the Frick. Central Park was a fabulous playground. I used to go to the theater and movies during the day and evening, often by myself. There seemed no end to the cultural offerings of the city.

I didn't really have enough training for any kind of a job and had no desire to get an advanced degree, since school was not my forte. That said, what *was* my forte? I had no idea. In college I had worked in the nursery school, but now that I had a child I wanted to branch out. I fantasized about being an anthropologist and living with some remote tribe in New Guinea, but the lack of academic training was an insurmountable obstacle.

One of my dates suggested that I become a hostess at a restaurant, with the responsibility of leading people to their tables. At the time I felt grateful that he thought there was something I could be paid for, but now I am quite indignant about his patronizing attitude.

I thought I might be able to get some interesting volunteer work and asked my father if he knew anybody I could talk to. He suggested I speak to his physician, Dr. Arthur Antenucci, who was the head of Roosevelt Hospital. Dr. Antenucci told me about a project the hospital oversaw at the Stratford Arms Hotel.

The Stratford Arms was a single-room occupancy (SRO) hotel in the West Seventies for elderly people who had been recently released from mental hospitals. It had a staff of social workers and an alcoholism counselor. The clientele was a mix of men and women who needed support and companionship. A nurse gave them their medication every day. I enjoyed working there and having interesting colleagues to share my experiences with.

I started out as a volunteer three days a week, and I was thrilled when Roosevelt Hospital put me on the payroll. My title was "Community Mental Health Worker." I was in charge of the sixth floor, in addition to handling a caseload of clients. There were several major problems on the sixth floor, and the residents were highly unstable, so calling an ambulance was fairly common.

One woman, an alcoholic, wouldn't bathe or clean her room. I tried to encourage her by getting her clean clothes and attempting to persuade her to shower. Finally I said—and I probably would be arrested for this now—"Today you are going to take a shower. We're going to do it together." I went into the shower with her, with my clothes on, and washed her all over, including her hair. I put her in clean clothes, and afterwards I went through her room, which made Grey Gardens look like Versailles and stunk up the whole sixth floor. I threw away the soiled rags that covered the floor and filled the closet. I cleaned up her room and stocked the closet drawers with fresh clothes. I left that afternoon feeling that I had actually accomplished something. When I returned the next day, one of the social workers told me that the woman had said, "Jeannette has imprisoned me in my clothes, and I can't get out of them." In a short time the new clothes looked like the old ones, and the closet and floor were once again covered with filth.

Another woman, named Marina, was very depressed. I'd bring in nail polish and lipstick (great healing remedies) and put make-up on her face and do her nails, which she liked. We went to her church together to light candles.

I also started a weekly reading group at the Stratford Arms. My father was interested in what I was doing, so he turned up at one session, and all the ladies fell in love with him. They kept asking me when he would return.

An elf-like woman with short gray hair lived at Stratford Arms and constantly made pronouncements. One day she gazed at me with her sparkly eyes, pointed a tiny finger, and capered around, saying in a tone of disdain, "You must have been one of them debutantes!" I wondered what made it so obvious.

Though I became very attached to the people at the Stratford Arms and stayed there for three years, the work wore down my spirit. The best I was able to do was maintain the status quo. Clients never seemed to move forward, no matter how hard we tried to help.

So when a position opened up at the Hayden Planetarium at the Museum of Natural History, I jumped at the chance. I thought the work would be both challenging and fun. My friend Tom Jones was working there as director of public relations, and I was brought in to start a council for young people who were interested in the planetarium. I had met Tom when my mother introduced us at the St. Regis Hotel. My parents and I were there to attend an awards dinner for my father, given by the Advertising Council. I jokingly asked my mother if she had a handsome single man for me. She immediately dashed off to introduce herself to the nearest attractive young man she saw, who happened to be Tom Jones, and asked if he was single. When he said he was, she dragged him back and introduced him to me, and we became good friends.

Happy to see one another at the party:
l. to r., Berry Berenson Perkins, photographer; Anthony Perkins, actor; Mrs. Osgood Perkins, actress; Robert La Chance, producer.

CELEBRATING A SEASON

The Planetarium marked the beginning of spring with a handsome "Stars of the Season" party held on March 20, the eve of the vernal equinox.

Beginning at 6 p.m., the party featured a wine-and-cheese reception plus a special sky show demonstrating how the heavens behave as the spring season begins.

The party was the first activity of a newly-formed group, the Planetarium Council. Its effectiveness under the leadership of Jeannette McElvenny, chairwoman, was evident from the $2580 it netted — a considerable increase over previous years. In addition, the party created great interest among an entirely new group of people, many of whom had not been in the Planetarium since their early teens.

Enjoying a conversation at the party:
Sir Humphrey Wakefield, antique dealer, with Jewelry designer and Mrs. Kenneth J. Lane.

Press coverage of the "Stars of the Season" party. I still went by the name Jeannette McElvenny.

The purpose of the council was to focus attention on the planetarium, dream up new programs, and raise money. Tom Jones and I went through our Rolodexes, and, among others, we invited three of my Miss Hall's friends—Allison Simmons, Prudy Painter, and Jocelyn Kress—and three from Sarah Lawrence—Jackie Bograd, Kathy Johnson, and Jane Stanton. We signed up my sister Olive, Kip Forbes (son of Malcolm), Lorna Livingston, the author and producer Chris Cerf, and Billy Hitchcock (son of the famous polo player). Diana "Mara" Henry took great photos at all our events.

I was not paid but loved the perks and prestige of my huge office in the basement of the planetarium. We tried to raise the profile of the planetarium with our "Stars of the Season" parties, which were tremendous fun.

George and Freddy Plimpton

Before each of our parties, Tom and I worked night and day to attract a high-profile crowd. We carried invitations with us everywhere, and handed them out whenever we saw someone who looked like a good candidate. We were thrilled when a man bought a ticket to one of the parties and we were told that he was the third-richest man in America. We even made up a song that started, "He is the *third*-richest man in America, not the first, no, no...."

Tom had an idea to create a "Star of the Season" award as a way of generating income and publicity. The concept was to organize an event around a well-known New Yorker who might have a connection to the planetarium. Freddy Plimpton suggested Lauren Bacall, since she lived at the Dakota, just seven blocks away, and had two young children. Freddy called Bacall and politely asked if she'd be interested. Her answer was not what we were hoping for. "What do I wanna go to a fuckin' party at the fuckin' planetarium for?" she graciously replied.

We also wanted celebrities to commit to attending, so that we could get pre-party publicity. Tom was a friend of Jane Perkins, the mother of Tony Perkins (of *Psycho* fame). So Jane, Tony, and his wife Berry Berenson (who later died on one of

Our team at the Planetarium. Front row, from left: Tom Jones, Kathy Johnson, Chris Cerf, Jeannette, Jackie Bograd, Henry Plimack, and Rae Crespin. Back row, from left: Kip Forbes, Lorna Livingston, George Beane, Allison Simmons, and Bill Murray. (photo by Diana Henry)

the planes that crashed into the World Trade Center) were regulars at our events. Freddy Plimpton was on our Planetarium Council, and she and her husband, the literary luminary George, were glamorous and newsworthy additions.

One of Tom's friends, Freddy Eberstadt, then a photographer (now a therapist), and his stunning wife, Isabel, the daughter of Ogden Nash, made a dramatic addition to our parties. Freddy suggested his friend Rachel Crespin might help us. Rae invented sportswear reporting at *Harper's Bazaar* and later had her own line of shearling coats sold at Bergdorf's and Saks.

She arranged for models to parade around at the party dressed in clothes designed by Bill Blass and Oscar de la Renta. One of the models stole a Bill Blass dress, so Tom and I had a lot of unwelcome excitement the next day.

Bill McMasters and Adolfo Garcia, two gifted decorators, designed the interior for our first party, stapling white fabric all over the planetarium, much to the consternation of the staff, who said it was a fire hazard but, in the end, grudgingly allowed it.

It was exciting to be on the periphery of the social world I used to read about enviously when I was in Grosse Pointe, and sometimes I was even in the columns myself.

The fortieth-anniversary party was perhaps our finest hour. Ivan Chermayeff, the well-known logo designer, came up with gorgeous blue invitations, and, to our happy surprise, Jackie Onassis agreed to be the chair of the benefit committee. It was the first time she'd lent her name to a benefit since the assassination, and every columnist in town called for details. Freddy and Isabel Eberstadt were on the committee, along with my parents. The party was held on October 9, 1975, the night of my thirtieth birthday. A lot of committee members hosted dinners beforehand, and the planetarium party ran from 9:00 p.m. to 1:00 a.m. My son Ralph recently reminded me that Salvador Dali brought Ultra Violet, one of Andy Warhol's "superstars," to my pre-party dinner. The dress code was "celestial," and the Guggenheim Space Theatre was transformed into a cabaret, with a wraparound slide show on the walls featuring photos of many of the guests, supplied by committee members. On the second floor we had a continuous laser show and disco. I had a wonderful time and stayed out extremely late. The next morning, my photo was in the paper and I was awakened by a ringing phone. I answered to an unknown male voice saying, "I saw your ass in the sky show last night." Ever polite, I said, "I'm sleeping now, can you call me back later?" Unfortunately he did. This time I hung up.

After one of our parties, a group of planetarium lovers from Philadelphia persuaded Tom and me it would be fun if we came to a big party on the Main Line. They organized a place for us to stay, and the party was an elegant hunt ball at someone's large house. (I recently asked Tom why we were invited, and he said it was for me to meet an "eligible" — a single man — but I have no memory whatsoever of meeting such a man.)

During the first course of dinner, the conversation began to remind me of Grosse Pointe, with talk about prominent local families and their social pedigrees. By dessert I was so bored I could hardly stay awake, and I pulled Tom into the house's small library to compare notes. It turned out Tom was having conversational difficulties himself. The woman next to him was talking to him about dog breeding. Thinking he could get a conversation going, Tom mentioned how much he liked pugs. His dinner partner gave him a withering look and said, "Not only do I know no one who breeds pugs — I know no one who owns one." Tom and I agreed we had to get out of there as soon as possible. Meanwhile I was checking out a box of chocolates, squishing the bottoms in search of the caramel and pecan ones I liked. At this point our hostess entered, looked at the chocolate box, and said angrily, "The children have been at the chocolate again."

When the hostess left, Tom picked up the yellow pages and started calling numbers until he found someone who could drive us back to the city. We invented a story about a sick relative we had to run home to, hastily said thank you and goodbye, and had our luggage ready by the time our getaway car appeared, an Econoline van. We were ecstatic to arrive back in New York at about three in the morning. The city had never looked better.

Another fundraising idea came from my friend Steven Aronson. He asked Patti Smith if she would be willing to give a concert under the dome of the planetarium. To clinch the deal, Jackie Bograd and I took Steven and Patti to lunch at Quo Vadis, an elegant restaurant on East Sixty-Third Street that has long since disappeared.

Jackie and I were seated, wearing our identical St. Laurent blouses, with lady-like bows at the neck. When Steven showed up at the table, he said the restaurant was keeping Patti outside because she, in a classic white men's shirt and jeans, did not meet the dress code. We managed to convince the maitre d' that Patti was a major celebrity, and thus not subject to the dress code for mere Upper East Siders.

Patti generously agreed to give a concert to benefit the planetarium, and I, careful of the conservative nature of the museum, suggested that we (meaning she) had to be a bit careful with the performance. Patti assured me that she knew how to behave for the "fancy people," and I was relieved.

The invitations went out and included a poem by Patti:

> Yum Yum the Stars are out tonight
> I'll never forget how you smelled that night
> Like feta cheese under fluorescent lights.

Tickets sold out in a flash, and soon the night arrived and a large audience was seated under the dome of the planetarium. Suddenly an image was projected on the dome: It showed Patti, seated on a toilet seat, ostensibly shooting up, while graffiti above her head read, "Patti's Pussy." I groaned and put my head in my hands, waiting for the plug to be pulled by angry trustees. Patty then acknowledged me, saying, "I'd like to thank Jeannette McElvenny: who did my hair tonight." (There was laughter from the crowd.) The concert continued to great acclaim. Everybody loved it, and I didn't lose my job. Luckily enough, none of the trustees came. I still remember it as one of the best concerts I ever went to. I remain a huge fan of Patti and every year look forward to her singing "People Have the Power" at the benefit concert for Tibet House at Carnegie Hall.

Chapter Twelve

After my divorce in 1972, I was ready to plunge into the '70s. I felt as though I had missed out on the swinging '60s, given my early marriage. New York was still buzzing with sex, drugs, and rock 'n' roll. I hadn't even heard the great rock bands, because my husband preferred Frank Sinatra. I began to listen to rock music and go to concerts. I told my friends I would love to meet some men, and I began dating. Even if I didn't particularly like some of my dates, I enjoyed their attention. I insisted that I was still getting over my divorce and was not interested in getting remarried.

That first Christmas of my single life I planned an elaborate rendezvous with the handsome German I had met at Prudy's wedding—and who had awakened in me the prospect of a freer, more exciting life. I rented a house in St. Moritz and invited Olive, Jocelyn, and Prudy and her new husband to join my son Ralph and me. When I arrived at St. Moritz, I took one look at my erstwhile suitor and realized he was not "The One." To his chagrin, I took Jocelyn as a roommate and assigned him a room in a galaxy far, far away.

Having Jocelyn as a roommate was a mixed blessing. I remember getting dressed one night in a black jersey dress, which I felt was quite becoming. Jocelyn, perched on the other twin bed, eyed me and then said, "You know, honey." Pause. "You really should wear a girdle under that dress." I instantly thought of Ring Lardner's great line—"'Shut up,' he explained"—and used those two words to silence Jocelyn.

Despite my non-romance, I had a wonderful time in St. Moritz. My father was friends with the owner of the Palace Hotel and got us memberships to the nightclub there, where we spent many lively evenings. Daddy also got passes for us to go to the exclusive Corviglia Club. It offered exceptional dining and every imaginable winter sport. It was chockablock with celebrities and titled members, many of whom Jocelyn seemed to know. One night at the Palace Hotel, Jocelyn spotted Andy Warhol and his business manager, Fred Hughes, and invited them to join us. I remember Andy was very quiet, occasionally saying, "Gee whiz." We made a date for another occasion, but this time Fred appeared without Andy. "He's in the room looking at a dog," he said. Later on in the conversation we started discussing money, and Fred said, "What good is money except for throwing out of backs of trains," an image I have always loved — and a practice in which I have, without meaning to, sometimes indulged.

The '70s were such an exciting time. It was as if all the promises of the '60s were being fulfilled. Women were liberated, schools were integrated, and equal opportunity was the watchword of the decade. Women had access to birth control and abortion. It was an opportunity for hedonistic pleasure before the specter of AIDS appeared. I turned up the volume of my Helen Reddy record and danced around my apartment singing, "I am woman, hear me roar."

I was interested in all the racy spots, including the Continental Baths and Plato's Retreat, a sex club where I went with a friend as a voyeur. Plato's Retreat was located in the basement of the Kenmore Hotel. Previously, the Kenmore had housed the Continental Baths, where Bette Midler used to sing. I remember walking down this narrow staircase to a central room that had a laid-out buffet like a college mixer's, with sliced meats and cheeses, white bread, and an open bar. The dance floor was clothing-optional, and a young preppy-looking nude couple was enthusiastically gyrating on the dance floor with lots of moving parts. My date and I danced nearby, sedately clothed, trying not to gawk. I remember wandering around the darkened sauna, seeing couples undulate on the floor. It was fun to go, as I had been very curious, but I felt no desire to participate. I told the author Christopher Coe about these experiences, and he incorporated the anecdote into his book *Such Times*, with some details changed to protect my identity:

"Last week a woman told me she had been [to the Continental] once or twice. She is not a woman I would have expected to go there. She is a married woman, a mother, runs a top photography gallery, is a social figure, always beautifully dressed, impeccably manicured, a woman with polish. Really, she is the last woman one would have expected to go."

Social conventions were changing so fast that I was getting confused about dating protocol. For instance, who should call? And who should pay? (Eventually I adopted my mother's old rule: Let the man make the first call and pick up the bill.) The old rules about sex no longer applied, and courtship seemed to have flown out the window.

My life and emotions seemed to be in a yo-yo state. Some of my relations with men took on an obsessive Proustian quality. I was alternately ecstatic over some wonderful evening or depressed that the object of my affection hadn't called back. I seemed to be drawn to men who treated me badly. Even though feminists claimed that women could enjoy sex in the same way men did—without attachment—I found this didn't work for me in the long run.

Fortunately, I had started analysis with an expert therapist who seemed likely to help me with my search for meaning in my life, for work that would be exciting and satisfying, and, of course, for love. I seemed to be drinking too much and hated the headachy, tired feeling I sometimes had in the morning. Adding recreational drugs made things even worse.

Five mornings a week, I would go in to Dr. Lester Friedman's office and lie down on the couch and talk. He responded from time to time, and I remember in particular his analysis of a dream I had. In the dream, I took the tram to Roosevelt Island with my 6-year-old son, Ralph, and everything there, from the trees to the apartments, was covered with cookies and candy. Dr. Friedman pointed out how emotionally starved I was to yearn for these rich sweets.

I became obsessed with one man even before we met, because of a photo I saw of him. By the time we met, I was already under his spell. We began a relationship in which our times together were bookended by long periods of no calls. I was alternately elated and miserable. One weekend, he invited me out to his beach house, and I was so nervous that I asked him to invite one of my sisters as well. On the Friday night of my arrival, I wasn't feeling well and went to bed early, with the uneasy feeling that Mr. X was paying too much attention to one of the other female guests. On Saturday I woke up, saw that it was a beautiful day, and decided I was imagining the whole thing. Two weeks later I went to El Morocco's with a group of friends and saw the other female guest seated at a table. She beckoned me over and then said loudly, "X spent Friday night with me and Saturday with you."

I was devastated and couldn't think of any Guermantes-style wit with which to respond. I was much calmer and happier once I was out of this masochistic relationship. Years later, my sister said he had made a pass at her as well.

Thirty years after this, I saw him on a flight back to New York from Detroit (where I had been visiting my first mother-in-law, with whom I remained close). He was as flirtatious as ever, but he had lost his allure. I couldn't imagine why I had once found him irresistible.

I met a charming, successful man who was very solicitous and had a gorgeous apartment. He took me out to expensive restaurants. One night he noticed I was a bit quiet. He said, "If I could wave a magic wand where would you like to be?" Without thinking I said, "At home. In bed. Alone," which, needless to say, I shortly was. Now I feel badly to have been so cavalierly rude to such a considerate man, but for some reason I told the truth.

A new acquaintance decided I would be a wonderful stepmother to her son and introduced me to her ex-husband, a handsome and interesting man. After our first date she called me to find out how it was. She was horrified to hear he had taken me to Brandy's on East Eighty-Fourth. At that time it offered all the food you can eat for five dollars. She immediately invited me out to an expensive French restaurant to make up for it.

Another man put me through a series of "tests." He took me to a party that his friends were giving and then basically dumped me while we were there. He later explained that he wanted to make sure I could deal with the situation. We continued to see each other (why, I don't know), and Christmas was coming. The big day arrived, and I got a call from one of my friends—a beautiful and worldly Italian woman. She said, eagerly, in her heavily accented voice, "Darling, vat did he give you? Gilberto giffs me gold jewelry, he giffs me French perfume." I was embarrassed to report that I had received a double boiler and a scrub brush from my less-than-ardent suitor, and the relationship broke up soon after.

One of my friends' fathers had a great saying about his daughter's suitors: "Only garbage flows to our shores." I felt it was flowing to my shores as well. Here I was, in my early thirties, and I still hadn't figured out what kind of life I wanted. Did I want to be married to an artist and live in a loft? Or have a very formal life in a gorgeous apartment with fancy restaurants amid the New York social scene?

I think the fact that I was reporting all this to Dr. Friedman every day made me think about my "relationships" and about what might make me happy. I began

LEFT: A night out with Brendan Gill (photo by Diana Henry)

RIGHT: With Brendan Gill after my hip surgery

to be able to appreciate men who treated me in a kinder and more respectful way. I wasn't "in love," however, and found I was happier on my own. I had a circle of friends who were happily married, with children around Ralph's age, and I enjoyed spending weekends with them in an atmosphere of easy domesticity.

I also had some wonderful male friends to go out with. Among the most engaging and amusing was Brendan Gill. Brendan was a writer for *The New Yorker*, a magazine that he loved and worked at for sixty years. His memoir, *Here at the New Yorker*, was a best-seller in 1975. He was my father's age and utterly unencumbered by political correctness, and his conversation was often hilarious. He was a student of architecture and worshipped Frank Lloyd Wright, about whom he wrote a biography. Brendan seemed to know who designed every building in the city, and a trip with him in a taxi was an architectural education.

He was the chairman of the board of the New York Landmarks Conservancy, and he and Jacqueline Onassis banded together to save Grand Central Station. He was a whiz at reciting Shakespeare and Yeats; he told me an uncle paid him for each line he memorized. Endlessly energetic, he took an early train every morning from Bronxville to Manhattan, worked all day at *The New Yorker*, and later went out, often until the early hours of the morning, before returning home to Bronxville. For several years he was the magazine's theater critic, and I accompanied him to many plays, after which he returned to *The New Yorker* and wrote his reviews.

Brendan came to visit me in Maine, and I drove him around to visit homes he was writing about for a book on summer houses, including the Dwight Morrow house, where Ann and Charles Lindbergh stayed before they took off in their seaplane from the Thoroughfare for their transpacific trip. Brendan became a friend of my father, who shared his interest in architecture. Brendan later had my father appointed as one of the judges for the Pritzker Architecture Prize. No one was more lively company than Brendan, and, along with many others, I deeply regret his death and feel that the city is a lesser place without him.

I also had my single girlfriends, who were often available for adventures at night, after I put my son to bed and left him with his nanny. Jackie's family was very generous, and I often ended up being taken out to dinner by her parents and her three sisters. If one of our boyfriends was going to a party, he ended up taking several of us along. My female friends were all around my age, and we were together so much that it was rumored we were gay. We didn't worry about getting married or having children, because we were having fun renting houses in East Hampton, taking trips to Maine, skiing in the winter, and dancing to tunes like "Lady Marmalade" at El Morocco's. I think we felt as though we would be young forever.

North Haven continued to be a big part of every summer, and it was quite an exciting place to be, due to my father's imagination. Daddy delighted in bringing back mementos from his travels—often huge ones. He was so fascinated by a log hut he saw in Switzerland that he had it transported back to Oak Hill Farm. His most unusual purchase was a Chinese junk from Hong Kong. We loved taking our sails in the only junk in Penobscot Bay.

~

In the spring of 1975, I traveled to Afghanistan with my father on a trip that we had been planning for a year. When I was eighteen, my father and I had read *Caravans* by James Michener, and we became intrigued with Afghanistan. Ten years later, my mother agreed to take care of young Ralph, and Daddy and I left on our adventure to South Asia. My father remembered that our trip had been spurred on by our pediatrician, Dr. Rodgers, who, after taking care of all six of us, decided at age sixty-five to leave Greenwich and go teach in an obscure hospital in South Afghanistan.

My father enlisted Charles Bennett of Afghan Airlines, Senator Chuck Percy, and Lowell Thomas to help us plan our trip. We each invited a friend along. He drafted George Simpson, a pal from Greenwich, and I took an old friend from Sarah Lawrence, Jane Stanton (soon to become Jane Hitchcock). My father was on the board of Pan Am, and the airline treated us extremely well and made sure we had a warm welcome in Iran, which was our first stop. We stayed at the Intercontinental Hotel in Tehran and were given large tins of caviar that I remember eating off my fingers. We visited the Shah's palace, which had a multitude of mirrors and ornate paintings and a magnificent throne encrusted with jewels. In thinking of this trip I remember so many good things about my father. He was a lot of fun to be with and a *super* traveler. The trip was all the more interesting because of his curiosity and zest for life.

We then flew to Afghanistan. Our guide, Durani, took us on an arduous sightseeing tour of Kabul. I was struck and horrified that so many women dressed in the burka, a covering even more restrictive than other veils I had seen—not even the eyes were exposed, just a little slit with netting over it. What my father enjoyed most about the day was "haggling on the street," as he called it. He was extremely pleased with the bargain he got on heavy rough Afghan socks, which I doubt he ever wore. The starting price was three dollars, but Daddy was able to get six pairs for ninety cents each. He got the same glee out of this as he got from driving free in and out of New York City on the Willis Avenue Bridge. I bought stone boxes inlaid with indigenous stones and also bracelets and necklaces to give away as gifts. Very presciently (this was in May of 1975), my father remarked on the large Soviet presence in Kabul, notably helicopters at the airport.

(Years later, President Carter appointed my father the U.S. ambassador to the Soviet Union. Alex and I arrived in Moscow for a Christmas visit and saw many tanks in the streets. When we woke up the next day, we learned that the Soviets had invaded Afghanistan. Later on, my father unofficially invited Andrei Gromyko to the residence and showed him some photos of the impenetrable mountainous terrain. Daddy said the minister of foreign affairs blanched at the sight.)

We later flew on to Bamiyan, which was a major caravan center for travelers from Russia, China, Lebanon, the Mideast, and Turkey. It had become a major tourist attraction because of the giant Buddhas carved into the sandstone cliffs

Jane Stanton and I check out the giant Buddhas in Bamiyan (photo by my father)

about 1,500 years ago. The Buddhas were headless, because, after Genghis Khan took over the area, ultra-devout Muslims decapitated them to remove their power. (It was heartbreaking when the statues were blown up and destroyed in 2001 by the Taliban, again as a supposed display of Muslim devotion.) I enjoyed climbing inside the Buddhas on steps cut into the stone. We were 8,000 feet above sea level, surrounded by the majestic snow-capped Hindu Kush. Watching farmers use cattle to plow their arid fields, we felt like time travelers who had stepped back a millennium.

After this, we drove to the Bandi Amir lakes, passing several camel caravans along the way. The six lakes are an extraordinary blue, because of their high mineral content. They are a breathtaking sight in the barren gray-brown landscape.

My father took stunning photos of nomads dressed in black, often with loose woven turbans. At night our "hotel" was a collection of comfortable yurts (circular tents on the ground with Western-style bathrooms nearby). My father told me he liked to get up early to walk around the camel markets, so the next morning we asked him to wake us, and we wandered to a market at around 5:00 a.m. Two young girls beckoned to Jane and me to accompany them, and we followed them into an inner courtyard where we saw a group of women, elaborately dressed in beautiful embroidered robes, sitting cross-legged on a platform that was covered with an ornate rug, drinking tea. They invited us to join them, and we managed to communicate warmly, despite not having a common language. Wherever we traveled in Afghanistan, the people were hospitable and friendly.

The trip gave me a taste for adventure trips, and I later went to Tibet, Peru, Myanmar and Bhutan. I am still hoping to someday see the reindeer people in Mongolia.

~

An Indian chief and shaman of the Banff Nation spent a summer with us carving a totem pole. My father had run across Chief Kitpou in Canada and thought him charming. He talked Daddy into letting him make a pole for us, and the chief and his assistant, Swoo whee ya, arrived with tools, costumes, and sacred objects for the dedication ceremony. Swoo whee ya, who was the son of another chief, had the "English hat name" of Michael Paul. I have no idea what an "English hat name" is, but evidently Chief Kitpou did not have one.

The chief cut quite a figure roaming Oak Hill Farm in his loincloth. He was shown several trees that our caretaker Jimmy Brown had selected. The chief had always carved dry trees, but decided to try one of these anyway. Before cutting it down, he and Michael Paul said a prayer, telling the old tree they would let it live again. They thanked the Great Spirit for the gift and filled the totem pole with love.

They used a chainsaw to carve the pole. The Indians build psychologically from God to Earth, from the eagle at the top to the whale at the bottom. The whale means all men are brothers. After the pole was completed, my father and the chief selected a spot where it would be seen not only from our property but also from the shoreline. The pole represented hospitality and was for all the children within fifty miles. My father was the guardian of the pole, and his name was carved under the whale at the bottom.

We had an elaborate ceremony after the pole was installed and invited neighbors and guests to join our family for the occasion. (Brendan Gill was totally intrigued by Chief Kitpou and insisted on calling him Winnie the Pooh.) The chief did some chanting and spoke about the pole. Then my father, Chief Kitpou,

CLOCKWISE FROM TOP LEFT: A sketch of the chief that his assistant, Swoo whee ya, gave to me
The author with Chief Kitpou
The Chief hard at work, wearing his loincloth
Chief Kitpou with his drum at the dedication ceremony (photo by Ross Meurer)

Michael Paul, and my son Ralph all sat in front of the pole and smoked a peace pipe. (Ralph didn't inhale.) Everyone held hands, and then the chief gave out gifts and taught us a war chant for the finale. My father later said he viewed Chief Kitpou's handiwork as a monument to fast-talking salesmen everywhere.

Years later, Chief Kitpou returned. I felt this was a wonderful opportunity for Ralph to absorb some ancient Native American wisdom, and I encouraged him to spend time with our loincloth-clad artist of the chainsaw. One rainy day, Ralphie slipped off to Chief Kitpou's R.V. where he stayed for several hours. Curious as to what was happening, I crept up and peeked through the window. Imagine my disappointment when I saw they were sitting side by side, watching television.

My father told me that by embellishing the property with animals, a log hut, the totem pole, and idiosyncratic junk, he was creating a "grandchildren trap." He made a special little path around the property filled with gnomes and other surprises. This was called the "grandchildren walk." Fifty years later, the property is still a grandchildren trap and, now, a great-grandchildren trap as well.

My parents had a steady stream of weekend guests flown in from Westchester Airport. Ann and Moose Taylor, from Colorado, came every year. Ann was on the best-dressed list, and I remember watching her husband stagger under the weight of her luggage. Once she arrived, it was expected that the "household staff" would unpack. Our housekeeper and our laundress from North Haven had never done this before, but they enjoyed looking at the beautiful clothes, as did I!

Many other prominent guests arrived over the years, including Lady Bird Johnson, Arthur Sulzberger, President Jimmy Carter, Dillon Ripley, Lowell Thomas, Walter Cronkite, G. F. Kennan, and Chuck and Lorraine Percy. At one point Senator Percy and I were in the galley of the *Palawan* creating sandwiches. He told me his favorite was crunchy peanut butter, sliced bananas, and honey on top. This remains my favorite as well! Malcolm Forbes liked to come on his mega-yacht, the *Highlander*, and he usually appeared every summer. He could be quite determined, as I discovered one visit. I had gone to have dinner with my parents while he was visiting. Mr. Forbes invited Alex and me to join my parents for lunch on board the *Highlander* the next day. We were planning a romantic picnic, but he insisted, and so we ended up on a glorious Maine day eating a lengthy formal lunch in his dining room—a heavy meal with wine and many courses, instead of our planned picnic on a secluded island.

A family gathering next to one of my father's antique planes (photo by Ross Meurer)

I remember President Carter as an extremely kind and gentle man. I will never forget how lovingly he looked at his wife Rosalyn when she entered the room. It was as though the sun had come out after months of rain!

Every summer Bobby and Teddy Kennedy and their families visited while cruising along the Maine coast. My mother never knew when they would arrive or how many guests they would bring. Oftentimes four to six more people than she had anticipated showed up. One summer they brought along Andy Williams, then married to the glamorous Claudine Longet. He told us about the show *Doctor Doolittle* and sang a song from it called "Talk to the Animals." Rosie Grier, a star lineman for the New York Giants, came several times, as did astronaut John Glenn. Olive taught John Glenn to drive a Model T, and she said she must not have been a good teacher, because he veered off the road and hit a tree after her lesson.

The Kennedys never sat still for a minute. They played touch football, swam in the ocean, rode horses, played tennis, and on and on. At night they liked to play games like Sardines in a Box, in which one player hides and everyone who finds him or her crams into the hiding place too. After dinner one night, we were all sitting in the barn and one of the Kennedys—I think it was Ethel—looked at us

Returning from lunch with Malcolm Forbes: Alex is at the helm, seated next to my father. My mother is wearing the scarf. I am in a printed t-shirt between my son Ralph and sister Helen.

Bobby Kennedy on his yacht. (Photo inscribed to my parents.)

rather apathetic teenagers and said enthusiastically, "Show us the latest dances." None of us obliged—one of the few times the Kennedys didn't get their way. Elsie Morrison, who worked as a laundress and helper on our property for many years, was quite upset at one of their "jokes." My father was having cocktails by the swimming pool, dressed in a smart navy blazer and slacks, when one of the Kennedys found it amusing to push him into the water.

Another time, Bobby and his group needed to be picked up in Camden. Paul Walter, my father's boat captain, took the *Palawan* to fetch them. As the Kennedys prepared to board, Captain Walter noticed that Bobby was carrying a little dog. He said, "You're not getting into my boat with that dog." "Oh, yes I am," Bobby said, and climbed on board. At this point Captain Walter grabbed the dog and threw it in the water. Bobby dove in to rescue his pet and later got into the *Palawan* sopping wet and without the dog. (Some kind soul offered to bring the dog on the ferry, and the two were reunited in North Haven.) Captain Walter was a law unto himself!

One year Teddy Kennedy cruised up the Maine Coast and stopped off to visit my parents. I was invited to dinner, and my sister and I and our friends were seated at the "children's" table (even though I was twenty-seven) in our barn, while the more grown-up and prestigious group were seated with Teddy in the dining room. During dinner our group decided it might be fun to look in Teddy's room, just off where we were eating in the barn. I took a peek in his shaving kit and was fascinated to discover several bottles of amyl nitrate there: at the time amyl nitrate was a much-talked-about drug to enhance sexual experience. (Please don't ask me how I know these things.)

After dinner everybody joined together for grasshoppers, those creamy green drinks that taste like a Peppermint Pattie, and a game of Sardines in a Box. During the game Teddy asked me if he could see me after, and I thought it might be fun to invite him to my cottage for a drink. No sooner had we arrived than Teddy put his hand on my knee and asked, "How old were you when you started to enjoy sex?" I must have had too many grasshoppers because I replied, "You know, Teddy, it is interesting you should ask that question, as I was wondering what you were doing with all the amyl nitrate in your shaving kit." He looked furious (as well he might!) and then laughed.

Shortly afterwards, I drove him back to my parents' house. "What's going to happen now?" he asked. "Nothing," I replied and drove home chuckling.

When my father died, I was disappointed that none of the Kennedys called or showed up at the funeral. In addition to our hospitality over the years, my father had volunteered his plane to fly some of the Kennedy family to California after Bobby was killed. We thought of them as friends. But as Elsie Morrison, our summer laundress, observed about the Kennedys, "No please or thank you—none of them ever did."

In 1969, Oak Hill Farm played a diplomatic role for the State Department. The government was hoping to have a naval base in Thailand, and my father was asked if he would be willing to entertain the king and queen in Maine. My father instantly responded that he would be delighted to entertain the Thai royals. Only then was he told that he and my mother could not be present, because their highnesses wanted total privacy to relax.

Some privacy: In addition to the royal couple's retinue, the State Department and the government of Thailand each provided about sixty security people.

Every available house on the island was rented for the 120 extra people. Numerous limousines were hired. My parents inspected the house and left before the king, queen, and their retinue arrived, not to return until the royal party had departed. The Secret Service was everywhere, a helicopter was at the ready in the front yard, and a cruiser stood offshore.

Our caretaker Jimmy Brown had quite a few colorful stories to tell. Evidently one night, around 2:30 a.m., the Thai security and U.S security got into a fight, after heavy drinking, and Jimmy had to go separate them (not part of his job description). Another time, when Jimmy was taking the Royals out in a lobster boat to picnic on an island, the heir apparent, against Jimmy's edict, tried to swim to shore. Unaware of how cold the water would be, he started sinking, and Jimmy had to fish him out by his hair, preventing an international incident and a scuttling of the naval-base plan. Another time, the King and Queen went to town to shop, and everybody, thinking that they were being polite, didn't say a word. The King was quite insulted, so when they left on their cruiser, Jimmy made sure there was a crowd of people to wave them off. Elsie said the men dressed beautifully every night in their silk suits.

Before they left Oak Hill Farm, the king asked everybody who worked there to come to the courtyard and stand in a line. He walked down the line, shaking everybody's hand, and gave each of them a silver ring with Thai insignia and an envelope with one hundred dollars in it. Elsie was pleased to report that she

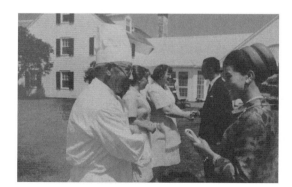

CLOCKWISE FROM TOP LEFT: The King and Queen of Thailand arrive in North Haven
The Thai royals outside our home in North Haven
Elsie with the king and queen
The Thai royals cruise the waters near our family compound

received an additional one hundred dollars from my father. The visit turned out to be a diplomatic success, because the U.S. Navy got a base in Thailand.

Years later, Alex and I traveled to Thailand, and I thought it would be fun to visit the palace. I wrote to refresh the king and queen's memory of their wonderful visit to our house in North Haven and said we would be coming to Bangkok shortly. Alas, the king's memory must have dimmed, since we never heard back. When I was younger, I tended to stay more on our family compound and invite guests to visit. Over the last decade, we have had fewer guests and have made wonderful North Haven friends. The social life is more interesting now than it was in the past, when the summer people and the islanders didn't mix much. Since then, many summer people have become full-time residents, and some have married islanders, blurring the distinction between the two groups. We have a world-class restaurant in Nebo Lodge, a beautiful inn, and a fabulous pizza restaurant in the village. Franklin's old grocery store has become Waterman's Community Center, a venue for children's programs, plays, and movies. North Haven is a wonderful place at all hours, especially for coffee and fresh doughnuts in the morning.

I have been coming to North Haven for over fifty years now, and with each passing season the island becomes more precious to me. Alex loves it as much as I do, and we spend more and more of our summers there. Nowadays I don't spend much time with my nose buried in a book, preferring to be out and about enjoying the beauty of the island. My mother used to joke that I became a "jock" with my biking, kayaking, and walking. Well, not quite, but North Haven has always been a bright spot in my life. When we return from the island, Alex and I often say to each other, "Why do we ever go anywhere else?" It's a joy when our compound fills up with family members, and I take special delight in my great-nieces and -nephews and our beloved grandson Henry.

Chapter Thirteen

During my seven years as a single woman, I gradually became more focused. I realized I would eventually like to remarry. I also was searching for a career that would be exciting and satisfying.

For me, the pieces were only partly in place. I had had my ring by spring, of course, and a child when I was twenty-three, but now I was divorced and at sixes and sevens about my career and romantic prospects. I enjoyed my work at the Planetarium Council, but when I was honest with myself, I knew what I was doing there wasn't fully satisfying. While the Planetarium was a good cause, I didn't think throwing parties to raise money was the best use of my talents, whatever they were. I also longed for something that would be my own and where I could create my own programs, with no stuffy Board of Directors looking over my shoulder. As for my love life, I enjoyed going out on dates (or at least most of them) and spending time with my friends and their families, but I longed for a deeper emotional attachment.

Then I encountered a bit of bad luck, and it turned out to be the best thing that had ever happened to me. It put me on the path to a career and a lifelong helpmeet.

When I was twenty-eight and skiing in Vail with my parents, they noticed I was limping and asked what was wrong. I said I had pulled a muscle. They convinced me to see a doctor, who told me I had congenital hip dysplasia — something I thought only afflicted golden retrievers. My father went with me to consult a number of doctors, because the procedure was complex and the recovery time was a year.

I ended up choosing a doctor at the Hospital for Special Surgery. As the day approached, I was terrified. My parents supported me by showing up early the day of surgery: my first of what would be seven hip surgeries! The doctor performed an osteotomy, removing a piece of bone at my hip so that the joint would fit better in the socket.

I woke up in pain and discovered the magic of morphine. I can see why people become addicted to it. I was at the hospital for two weeks and did quite a bit of entertaining in my room. At one point during my stay, I hired someone to do my hair and make-up, and I dressed up in a beautiful peignoir.

Then I went home for a lengthy recuperation—first on a walker, then on crutches, and finally with a cane. This took months and a lot of physical therapy. By the time I was walking on my own again, I had developed a limp, because my rejiggered hip made one leg a bit shorter than the other. Well-meaning friends would ask what was wrong, and I would snap back at them, "Nothing! Everything is great!" In truth, it was a big blow, because physical perfection was so highly prized in our family.

I was sustained by a dream I had had just before I went into the hospital. I was in a bookstore surrounded by books, hundreds of them. The store had two floors, and it was cozy and old-fashioned.

While recovering, I worked hard to make my bookstore dream become a reality. Steven Aronson was the only person I knew in the world of publishing. Steven was an old pal of my cousin Walker's, and we renewed our friendship when we rented houses next to each other in East Hampton. He was a co-publisher at Harcourt Brace Jovanovich. I invited him out for lunch and told him about my plans for a store that would be like a private home filled with books for serious readers. There would be book-related events, parties, and gallery openings. Steven was extremely encouraging and introduced me to people he thought could help, including some talented architects.

Gradually I found a partner and commercial space on Madison Avenue. I borrowed half of the start-up money from my father, who at first cautioned me against the plan. "How will you feel if you fail?" he asked. I took a night to think about it and then told him I would rather try and fail than not do anything. I later came across a quote by George Eliot that expressed my feelings more elegantly:

The proud bookseller (photo by Joyce Ravid)

"Failure after long perseverance is much grander than never to have a striving good enough to be called a failure." My father, happily enough, became one of the store's big boosters.

Burt Britton, who learned about the book trade at the Strand in the East Village, became my partner for the first year of Books & Co. We signed a fifteen-year lease for the first two floors of 939 Madison for $60,000 a year. Not only did we have a lot of construction work to do, we needed to come up with a name. My partner Burt wanted to call it Books. When my father and I were at lunch one day, he suggested it should be "Books & something." He wrote on the tablecloth "Books & Sympathy," "Books and ----." I woke up in the middle of the night and thought: "Books & Co. Books & Co." It was catchy, and the pun brought a smile.

I described our early days to Lynne Tillman for her book *Bookstore: The Life and Times of Jeannette Watson and Books & Co.*:

"Burt had brilliant ideas, one of which was to open the store with all the

Welcoming customers to Books & Co. (photo by Joyce Ravid)

books signed by their authors. I'd drive to outlets and pick up cartons of books, then we'd go to the writer's house to have them signed. The very first author we visited was Allen Ginsberg. We drove to Allen's apartment on East Tenth Street around a quarter to 12 at night. I yelled "Allen" at the top of my lungs. He threw down his key, and we walked up several flights of stairs. Burt had to carry all those boxes of his books up all those stairs. Ginsberg signed every book, and then, in a sweat, Burt had to carry all the boxes down. For a while I stored the books in my apartment, but once we had 939 Madison, and the space was ready to receive them, we brought the books there. There were many, many signed books in my apartment.

"Then they had to be shelved, and Burt's friends helped out. Burt excited people about the bookstore. He was so charismatic, he could charm well-known writers even into shelving books. Alice Trillin, Harold Brodkey—they were there, helping out, eager to see the store thrive. Ellen Schwamm helped, too, and she met Harold Brodkey while shelving books. One night, Ellen invited every-one working in the bookstore for dinner, and it was that very night when Ellen

The second floor of Books & Co. (photo by Joyce Ravid)

fell madly in love with Harold. She left her husband and went off with him. Ellen had once taken a class with Anatole Broyard, who thought Harold was one of the greatest writers ever, so she was in love with him, in a sense, even before she met him.

"Burt and I agreed on how the store should look, on getting as many books as possible signed, on what books should be in the store. Our mantra was literary fiction, poetry, and signed books. Books & Co. was going to be a writer's hangout. Initially I wanted to separate women writers from men writers, shelve Jane Austen and George Eliot and the Brontës in one section, but Burt said, "No, a writer is a writer; they should all be together." He was right.

"I wanted to allow for a certain kind of experience, for discovery, I wanted Books & Co. to be a salon. So the store had to have a specific look. I knew what that was—it had to look the way it did in my dream: cozy, comfortable, lived in. I remember going with Brendan Gill to the Customs House, where I bought bookcases and vitrines. They contributed to its look of being a nineteenth-century bookstore."

Burt greatly expanded my reading by sharing with me his favorite books. Soon I was reading and loving *The Assistant* by Bernard Malamud, *Invisible Cities* by Italo Calvino, and *The Dead of the House* by Hannah Green. These were followed by *The Moviegoer* by Walker Percy, *Keep the River on Your Right* by Tobias Schneebaum, and many others. Starting Books & Co. made me feel more confident and secure—and less dependent on the men I was dating.

Then, one lovely Saturday afternoon in June, I had an invitation to attend my cousin Liz's wedding. That morning I thought to myself, "Maybe I won't go,

I already have a date for the night." But then in my mind's eye I heard my mother saying, "You *have* to go to the wedding, you never know who you might meet." I knew she was right, so that night, dressed in a '30s-style flowered chiffon Jackie Rogers dress, I found myself wandering around the River Club ballroom, having a good time greeting relatives and friends. As I walked across the dance floor I saw a tall, dark, and handsome young man with large brown eyes coming toward me. He said, "Aren't you Jeannette Watson?" Turned out, we had met years ago at Fishers Island, when I was fourteen and he was twelve. I didn't notice him because he was so young. At that point two years make a big difference. His name was Alexander Sanger, and six months later he would be my husband.

We'd actually first met one spring vacation at a hotel in Naples, Florida, where our families were staying. I was six and he was four. We overlapped again at Fishers Island, where the Sanger family summered, and I *still* didn't notice him. He claims that he'd always had a crush on me. We were in a Junior Lifesaving Class together, and one afternoon a whole bunch of us took the ferry to New London to see *Psycho*. Alex persists in calling this our first date. It turns out he was also at the Patti Smith concert at the Planetarium.

At thirty-two, I was certainly ready to notice a tall, dark, and handsome thirty-year-old man. He was a wonderful dancer, and we had fun at the wedding. Alex took me home, but we both had plans for the evening. He said he would call, and on Monday morning the phone rang. I was at the bookstore, which hadn't opened yet. It took me a while to find the phone, buried under a mound of books. When I finally answered, it was Alex, calling to ask me out.

I remember thinking at first that he would be perfect for my friend Allison. Thank goodness I was in analysis, working through my depression. As I lay on the couch relating stories about Alex to Dr. Friedman, I realized (with a bit of guidance) that Alex was too good to give away, and that I should get to know him. Alex is a gentleman in the best sense and has always treated me with old-fashioned courtliness, which I deeply appreciate. After thirty-eight years of marriage, he still opens the car door for me. When we were dating, I loved being called, picked up, and taken on interesting outings— and I still do! Unlike my mother I did not want a caveman! At this point Alex was working as a lawyer in the trust and estates department of White & Case. He had long hours and occasionally had to cancel our dates at the last minute.

Sailing with Alex on the *Palawan*

On our first "date" I put him to the test. I was busy the night he invited me out but suggested he come along. My friends Kathy Johnson, Jackie Bograd, and I had all been invited to a Sarah Lawrence event at a beautiful town house on the Upper East Side. I was eager to see what my friends thought of Alex. After the party we ended up at Elaine's restaurant, where we had a lively time, while wine flowed freely. Alex was the only one to order dessert. He was horrified to find his dessert scarfed up by the three of us before he had a forkful. He also wound up paying the bill for me, plus three others.

Undeterred, Alex kept inviting me out, always changing the venue to keep things interesting. He'd take me to a lovely French restaurant on the Upper East Side, and then to a diner on Tenth Avenue. I loved the variety, which was matched by Alex's conversational interests. One rainy day he arrived at my apartment with a blender and all the makings for banana daiquiris. A dreary day became happy and fun.

Shortly after I met Alex, I went lingerie shopping at Bergdorf's. As I started gathering beautiful lacy and beribboned underwear (a lot of black), the clerk said to me "Oh, are you getting married?" "No," I responded, "I'm starting an affair!"

The Bee Gees were a popular group at the time, and I remember their song "More Than a Woman" was playing the first time Alex kissed me.

After meeting Alex: Nothing like romance to make a girl smile.

I invited Alex to North Haven for a weekend, which was the sternest test yet. Would he like it? Would my family and friends like him? Would Alex feel at home in rustic North Haven after all those summers at Fishers? My father provided his plane and a pilot to take us from Westchester to our airstrip in Maine.

Alex loved North Haven. I think my parents were relieved that Alex was obviously a "Suitable Boy." He played tennis with my sisters, sailed, and took us out in the motorboat. It seemed there was nothing he couldn't do. He even carried a Boy Scout knife, in keeping with the organization's slogan: "Be prepared!"

My friend Jackie was very impressed with Alex when we got caught on a lobster pot while out on our boat. Alex stripped to his underwear and dove in the water, Boy Scout knife in hand, to cut us off, and then retied the lobster pot.

I divided my guests for the weekend into three teams of two to do the cooking. On Saturday night, Alex and his partner decided they would grill a butterflied leg of lamb. They went to Waterman's, our local grocery store, but Franklin didn't butterfly his legs of lamb. No problem for Alex. He had managed to pick up some carving skills from his surgeon father and deftly butterflied the lamb himself. After marinating the lamb in a yogurt sauce, Alex grilled it to perfection: pink inside and crusty outside. The pièce de résistance was the crème brûlée he made for dessert. By the end of the weekend, we were all smitten with him.

The only problem was geography. Alex was helping to launch the White & Case office in Palm Beach, and I was only interested in living in New York, particularly now that my bookstore was about to open.

Alex had been divorced for two years. He was living with a group of friends in a lovely town house on the Upper East Side. I did not enjoy spending the night there, because one bathroom served about three bedrooms. And as much as I liked Alex's friends, I wasn't eager to see them early in the morning. When I saw Alex's room, I was impressed by its neatness and also by the fact that he had a plant that looked healthy. Subliminally I must have thought that if he could take care of a plant, he could take care of me.

He had been studying ballet, an ingenious way to meet girls, because very few straight men were taking classes. He was also going to cooking class, and one night he announced he would cook dinner for me. I remember the meal vividly. We started with oysters in champagne sauce, then fish in parchment, and, for the finale, a homemade chocolate cake. I recently said to Alex, "You haven't made your chocolate cake in thirty-five years." He jokingly responded, "I haven't needed to." Then he relented and created the same cake, which was just as delicious as I remembered it.

The summer of 1978 was an extremely happy and exciting time for me. My bookstore was about to open, and my romance with Alex was proceeding apace. I felt he would make a wonderful husband for me and a caring stepfather for young Ralph. In November, shortly after the opening of Books & Co, Alex took me to Central Park and asked me to marry him. I was thrilled to accept and called my parents to report the happy news. As I was telling them that Alex and I were planning to throw our own reception, my mother interrupted: "I would love to give the reception for you." I pointed out that she had already given me a lavish wedding and reception. She replied she was happy to give each daughter two weddings. Given that she had five daughters, this was quite a generous offer! Later I realized that, between the five girls, there were indeed ten weddings.

I did have one caveat for Alex: I told him I could never be married to a man who hadn't read *Pride and Prejudice*. He read it and loved it. Years later we took a course at the Y and read Jane Austen's complete works together.

The autumn flew by, as I divided my time between Books & Co and planning our wedding reception. Alex was already in Palm Beach, renting a charming

'50s he joined the Marines, had a brief marriage, then decided to try acting. ("In Brooklyn, how the hell else do you meet girls?") At 23, he came across Faulkner's *The Hamlet.* "I read 30 pages and said, 'My God.' " The experience changed his life.

"I drove a cab and bartended nights so I could live in bookstores," Britton says, and finally he got a job at the Strand. "I gave my life to that place. In 10 years I went out to lunch seven times."

Agreeing that the last thing New York needed was another book supermarket, Burt and Jeannette launched their enterprise by ordering duplicates of all the great books he had hoarded in his apartment. The Wall is fast filling up, but Britton still spends hours harrying inefficient publishers to deliver the volumes he has ordered. "What should I do?" he fumes. "Go to their warehouses with a tommy gun?"

Having done "incredible" holiday business, Burt seems almost dubious

Burt (above) complains, "I haven't been to the movies since we opened." Co-founder Jeannette reads Jane Austen to relax.

about the hurly-burly of commercial success. "I'd like to lock the doors," he muses, "and live here by myself." Jeannette, who married Wall Street lawyer Alexander Sanger at Christmastime, seems more reconciled. "This is the wave of the future in bookstores," she says. "Back to the 19th century."
—HARRIET SHAPIRO

Photographs by Jill Kromentz

In the early days of Books & Co. with Burt Britton

little house with its own pool. We alternated weekends between New York and Palm Beach and hoped the White & Case office would bring him back to the city soon. But after seven years of living alone, this was a good way to ease back into marriage.

Alex and I shopped together on Palm Beach's Worth Avenue for the dress that I would wear to our reception: not a wedding dress but a pretty gold-and-silver cocktail dress. I love the fact that we were married on the winter solstice in 1978, the deepest and darkest day of the year.

We did not have a formal wedding but had a State Supreme Court Judge come to my parents' apartment. He was extremely late, and I was very upset. When I cooled off, I wondered why I cared if I was married or not for the reception. We

A wedding dance with Alex at the River Club

could have easily married the next day. We had a brief civil ceremony. Alex read a stanza from "Renascence" by Edna St. Vincent Millay, one of my favorite poets, in which she describes the view from Camden toward North Haven:

> All I could see from where I stood
> Was three long mountains and a wood;
> I turned and looked another way,
> And saw three islands in a bay.
> So with my eyes I traced the line
> Of the horizon, thin and fine,

When the ceremony was over, my parents, friends, and family left my parents' apartment to go down to the River Club ballroom to greet our guests and dance to the music of Mike Carney.

Alex's family was all there, and my niece Katherine, seeing Alex's three tall, dark, and handsome brothers, said, "Which one is Jeannette's husband?" The evening was fun, fairly informal, and relaxed. We left the party around 8:30 and headed off to the St. Regis for our wedding night. Alex had arranged for flowers, champagne, and, best of all, Häagen-Dazs ice cream and brownies from Greenberg's on Madison Avenue, which made the most sinful desserts in the city. It was an extremely happy time. We spent the whole next day together and went ice skating at Rockefeller Plaza, and that was our honeymoon.

Christmas was less than a week away, and December is the biggest retail month, so it was back to the bookstore for me! The place was hopping. I was thrilled to see the long lines of people at the cash register, holding their stacks of books. I always enjoyed the excitement and bustle of Christmas at Books & Co., especially helping customers select their gifts. We lavishly decorated the store and gave wine and cookies to our favorite customers, creating a festive atmosphere. By 6 p.m. on the Saturday before Christmas, our customers had gone home to their families, and Alex drove over to pick me up—something he did every year for the twenty years that Books & Co was in business.

I left the bookstore amid swirling snowflakes and the gorgeous Christmas decorations on Madison Avenue. I was so excited to be starting my new life with a man I trusted and loved.

Chapter Fourteen

That was a long time ago, a lifetime ago — the start of a new life, really. Alex moved in with me and my son, Ralph, at my apartment at 7 Gracie Square. I went to my bookstore every day, and Alex went to his law office at White & Case on Wall Street. It was a busy life for me, between work and family. Young Ralph soon had two little brothers, Andrew and Matthew. I joined several boards, including The Landmarks Conservancy and The Academy of American Poets.

Books & Co. was an exciting place to go every day. I loved looking at the catalogues with my sales reps, many of whom became friends, and helping to choose what books to order. The sales reps knew the kinds of books that would be right for Books & Co. I'd get galleys of the hot new titles and was invited to parties and lunches to meet authors. I impressed my children when I took them to a party for Michael Crichton at the Museum of Natural History. His agent, Lynn Nesbit, kindly introduced him to my children, who were thrilled to shake his hand. My youngest said he would never wash his hands again.

To be surrounded by so many fascinating books was a childhood dream come true. The excitement of new titles arriving was matched by the buzz created by our high-profile clientele. My children loved hearing about the celebrities who dropped by, including Bill Murray, Dustin Hoffman, Meryl Streep, Robin Williams, and Woody Allen. Hoffman did a spontaneous reading of *The Snake* by D.H. Lawrence, and Williams did a Barbra Streisand imitation for me by the cash

Our three boys: Matthew, Ralph, and Andrew

register shortly after the opening of his movie *Mrs. Doubtfire*. Woody Allen used the front of the bookstore in a movie.

One day I was in the back of the store when someone came back and told me Paul McCartney was in the store. I raced to the cash register and pushed whomever was there aside so I was ready to ring up his order. He came up, books in hand, and I noticed that he had chosen all his books from my table of recommendations. I said, "Oh, you've chosen all my picks..." He responded, "Yes, and if I don't like them, I'll come back and talk to you about them." (I inwardly thought, "I hope he doesn't like them," as he was as adorable as I remembered.) He followed by saying, "I just read a book I didn't like." I asked which one, and he replied "*Moby Dick*." I agreed heartily and said, "Biggest yawn in the world." Brendan Gill had insisted I read it years before, and I was quite embarrassed that I didn't love it the way everybody said I should have.

Truman Capote came in often in the first few years. He'd ask "Do you want to go to the Carlyle?" and we'd run away to Bemelman's Bar—my favorite bar in the city. As expected, he loved to gossip and was a great storyteller. Truman showed me the announcement of Lee Radziwill calling off her wedding and said in that funny high-pitched voice of his, "I sent her a very expensive wedding present. I hope I can get it back."

Another time we were discussing some well-known society woman, and he said, "She looks as though she was made up by the chief beautician at Frank Campbell's."

So many of my literary heroes—Octavio Paz, Robertson Davies, and Shirley Hazzard, among them—came in to buy books and sign their own. Carlos Fuentes met my young son Ralph while visiting me in my office. Ralph asked him if he believed in ghosts. "Not only do I believe in them," he said, "I write books about them."

Often the writers would run into their friends, and I would introduce them to customers, so the store became the kind of salon I had dreamed of. I got a special thrill out of discovering first novels and still remember my excitement when Susannah Moore walked in right after I had finished *My Old Sweetheart*, which I loved. I took her upstairs to sit on the green sofa and tell me all about her exotic Hawaiian life.

My parents often invited us to come "home" to Greenwich for holiday meals or Sunday lunches, triggering some of my old anxieties. I was careful about what I said to my father, in hopes of keeping things calm. Just when I thought I was doing a good job, he would have one of his eruptions. "But, Daddy, I thought we had been getting along so well?" I'd say. "*I've had to bite my tongue!*" was his emphatic response. As always, though, we also had some wonderful times.

During the summer in North Haven, we sailed on my father's yacht and had cookouts, and I was grateful that he showed such an interest in my children. He took Ralph on various adventures, and drove Andrew and Matt in his Model T to buy ice cream. He created a "grandchildren walk" around the property—a lovely path going from "The Big House," as we called it, to our homes, so his grandchildren could visit him without going on any road with cars. He decorated the path with ceramic gnomes to entertain the children.

I often had fun with my mother, going out to lunch or chatting by the swimming pool in Maine where she did her aqua exercises. I still wished I could regale her with stories of dances where every man tried to cut in on me, but that was her life, not mine. The bookstore didn't much interest her, and she rarely stopped by.

On the surface, my life seemed perfect, but I continued to have bouts of depression and no effective coping mechanisms. Alex was always wonderfully supportive, and his presence was a huge comfort. But depression is a psychological disorder with no easy cure. It would envelop me without warning, making me feel that I was an observer of my life, not a full participant. James Joyce described my feelings perfectly: "Mr. Guppy lived a short distance from his body."

I lacked self-confidence and often refrained from expressing my opinions to authors for fear of seeming stupid. I also felt inadequate as a mother. Sometimes I was too depressed to be fully present for my children. Because my own childhood had been so unhappy, I wanted to protect them from any unhappiness, which of course is impossible. Sometimes I would come home from the bookstore and lie on my bed, too emotionally debilitated to be with them.

So much of my life had been about learning to be happier, and I was willing to try anything. Around the time I married Alex, I discovered The Open Center, the largest holistic learning facility in the country. The Center had a wonderful instructor of Tibetan Buddhism, Gelek Rimpoche. One thing he said still resonates after all these years: "Anger is the single most negative emotion you can feel. It will not only hurt you in this life but in all your future lives to come."

I learned about training my mind and staying in the moment: not torturing myself with past failures. I have been lucky to have some great teachers, including Galek Rinpoche, Lama Yesshe, and Ashok Rinpoche. Buddhism seems so practical to me; it teaches wonderful methods for dealing with fear, anger, depression, and other negative emotions. I carry in my wallet a tiny green book called "The 37 Practices of a Bodhisattva." If I feel my mood shifting, I open it randomly and find helpful information. Recently I opened it randomly to #11, which starts, "All suffering without exception comes from wishing for one's own happiness." My meditation practice has become more regular, and I find it very helpful.

Through the people at the Open Center, I heard about Robert Thurman. At the request of the Dalai Lama, Thurman and other notables, including Richard Gere and composer Philip Glass, founded Tibet House, which is dedicated to preserving Tibet's art, culture, and spiritual heritage. Tibet had been a source of deep fascination to me since my teens, when I read *Seven Years in Tibet* by the Austrian mountaineer Heinrich Harrer. Professor Thurman (the father of actress Uma Thurman) was a Buddhist monk for a while and a translator for the Dalai Lama. He later became a professor in Tibetan Studies at Columbia.

A friend of mine was on the board of Tibet House, and when she heard about my interest she proposed me for the board as well. At one of my first Tibet

Bob Thurman and our group on a temple top (photo supplied by Bicky Kellner)

House board meetings, Professor Thurman announced that he was leading a trip to Tibet the following week. I begged to be allowed to come and was somewhat surprised when he said, "Yes, if you can get your papers in order." I raced home, invited my dear friend Bicky Kellner to accompany us, and scurried to get my visa together, leaving Alex to hold down the fort.

My trip with Professor Thurman—now known to me as Bob—was a transformative experience. The flight over the Himalayas to Lhasa was breathtaking, and my heart beat faster as I repeated to myself: "I am at the roof of the world." Bob spoke fluent Tibetan, and we heard many sad stories from the people we met. Buddhism, with its emphasis on staying in the moment, helped Tibetans find joy in life, despite their horrendous living conditions. They were resilient, spiritual, and beautiful.

Every morning Bob would give us a Buddhist teaching. In Lhasa we sat on a temple roof, gazing at the Patola Palace, while Bob extolled the merits of becoming enlightened. "Bob, I can understand how it would help me to become enlightened," I said, "But how would it help others?" He replied, "You know how the Dalai Lama is a giant Bliss Blaster? You could be like that..." I came home, continued to practice Buddhism, and have been trying to blast bliss ever since.

Professor Thurman in discussion with a monk (photo by Bicky Kellner)

A few years after the Tibet trip, I took another spiritual journey. I became obsessed with the idea of going to Medjugorje after reading an article about it in *Normal Magazine.* The article described a small remote town in Yugoslavia where many people believed the Virgin appeared daily to a group of six children: this phenomenon had transformed the village, and people were being healed. I was fascinated. "Would you mind if I went?" I asked Alex. He said it was fine, as long as I didn't become a nun.

I found my stay in Medjugorje interesting. I was disappointed to find the town so different from the way I had imagined it: Medjugorje had become more like Graceland than Jerusalem — not exactly what I had in mind when I set out! I did have an amazing opportunity to observe one of the visionaries named Ivan, in a small room with an altar and a crucifix and many priests. My guide told the head priest I was a reporter for *New York* magazine, and I was brought in. Ivan stood up, made a special prayer to Mary, and, for around ten minutes, gazed at the wall, while he seemed to be speaking with the Virgin. He nodded his head and moved his lips in response. Although I was somewhat disappointed that he did not have a more ecstatic expression on his face, I believe he was sincere. To me, the phenomenon was a mystery, although I believe the priests and Ivan believed in the miracle.

Because we had young children, Alex and I wanted a spiritual home for our family. We joined All Souls Church, partly because Unitarianism didn't demand much in the way of doctrinal belief, and partly because it gave people a chance to explore ideas and think about how to live. I no longer believed in the Christian faith I had been taught growing up. I didn't accept the existence of hell or the idea of original sin. Too much "God" talk began to get on my nerves. For a while, All Souls was a wonderful place for our family, but later on there was a huge rift in the church, when it became known that the minister was having an affair with his chief fundraiser—at the same time that he was providing marriage counseling to her and her husband. Alex and I felt so strongly about the church that we took a leadership role in opposing the minister. Everyone makes mistakes, but he never seemed to realize that what he did was wrong, nor did he sincerely apologize. Ultimately we decided to leave the church.

For the first ten years, Books & Co. did well, but gradually it started to lose money. When I renewed our fifteen-year lease, the Whitney doubled our rent to $120,000 a year. Thanks to our high rent and the advent of the superstore and discounted books, our losses increased each year. I felt after twenty years that I couldn't continue.

After my career as a bookseller ended, I felt as though I had lost my identity. I had no more galleys to read, no more glamorous parties to attend, no more calls from journalists. I missed the excitement of opening our glass-mullion-and-mahogany door at 939 Madison and entering my own Oz. Many authors disappeared from my life, because I no longer was important in promoting their books. I desperately missed the customers with whom I had become close over the previous twenty years. I had come to know their literary tastes and was always thrilled when they returned to say how much they enjoyed a book I had suggested. I also missed the bright young people I worked with.

The last year was all the more stressful because of the uncertainty and drama. Many people were protesting to the Whitney about our high rent, and several potential backers came and went. My hopes were raised and lowered several times. By October 1997 I knew that our negotiations with the Whitney were not working out, and I prepared for my last Christmas at Books & Co. My thoughts strayed toward my wardrobe (as they often do). I always wore red in December, or bright pink or purple—sort of advent colors. Bright colors cheered people up when they were weary with shopping. That Christmas, knowing what I had to announce afterwards, bright colors were necessary to cheer me up as well.

It was hard to give up a life combining so many things I enjoyed: people, books, interesting conversation, and also a certain prestige. I woke up each day to what I felt was a colorless, purposeless existence. At Books & Co. all I had to do was walk in the door and the magic began. After Books & Co. closed, the movie *You've Got Mail* with Meg Ryan and Tom Hanks came out. It was about a small independent bookstore closing after a Barnes & Noble–type store opened nearby. I was told some of it was based on all the articles written by Ron Rosenbaum in the *New York Observer* about Books & Co.'s demise. The movie started off with Meg Ryan opening the gate protecting the front of the window of the bookstore. I started weeping, saying to Alex, "I used to open the gate at Books & Co." I continued to sniffle all the way through. I even identified with a scene in which, after her store has closed, Meg Ryan's character finds herself falling into bookselling mode in someone else's bookstore. This happened to me as well.

Without Books & Co., I became terribly depressed. I felt I had nowhere to go and nothing to do. I spent hours in our basement storage room, going over my archives and remembering the good times. Soon I was so depressed that I spent Thanksgiving weekend in my pajamas, mainly in bed. Eventually I realized that it wasn't healthy to keep living in the past. I called the New York Public Library to see whether they might be interested in my papers. Ultimately the papers were accepted by the library's Manuscripts and Archives Department; they now reside in a kind of wire-cage storage bin, not too far away from George Washington and his recipe for beer.

Ned O'Gorman, knowing I was at loose ends, called and asked if I would like to help out at his new school in Harlem: The Ricardo O'Gorman School and Library.

Ned was a charismatic man and a poet who had started The Children's Storefront School in Harlem in the mid 1960s. I eventually published his collection of poems, *Five Seasons of Obsession*, under my Books & Co. imprint. He used to bring groups of children to visit me at Books & Co. Ned would come in like the Pied Piper with six or seven joyful children, who would race upstairs to the children's section and enthusiastically look through the books. We would end the visit with my reading a story, with some adorable child on my lap.

Ned had left the Children's Storefront School, which he founded amidst acrimony and notoriety. I wrote a letter to Elsie Aidinov, on the school's board, chastising her for letting Ned go. Later on, after years of experience with Ned, I came to agree with Elsie that he was difficult to work with and called Elsie to apologize.

Ned (with hat) on top step (photo by Joyce Ravid)
With Ned O'Gorman (photo by Joyce Ravid)

I have never seen a more wonderful learning environment than Ned's school. We had three-, four-, and five-year-olds with excellent teachers. I remember that the children were learning Chinese calligraphy, and I was so impressed by how much they remembered each time. We would take the children on outings. Ned loved the Metropolitan Museum of Art; with children in tow, we would proceed upstairs to the Japanese teahouse, which we all loved, as there were goldfish in a tiny pond. Or we might wander in Central Park and go to the children's favorite rock.

I also joined the board of directors of the school, which was a challenge, to say the least. Many of us left the board. Ned once brought all the parents out of his school to protest at one of his own board meetings.

Ned had a provocative fundraising technique. At one point he asked me for money, and as he didn't think the check I sent was enough, he ripped it up and sent it back to me with a note saying, "I guess IBM isn't doing too well."

I loved teaching kindergarten again, which I hadn't done since I studied early childhood development at Sarah Lawrence.

Ned was one of the truly great people I have known. He was able to transform the lives of so many children with passion and devotion. Many people started out in Harlem in the '60s, but Ned stayed the course and followed his destiny.

Epilogue

W hat are you planning to do now?" my sister Lucinda asked me.
"I don't know, maybe I'll become a healer," I said. This thought came
to me out of the blue, or, more precisely, from my unconscious. It changed my
purpose in life. Running a bookstore was eminently respectable, even prestigious. Now I was embarking on a career that often causes dinner partners to turn
quickly away rather than discuss something that strikes them as weird or - kiss of
death—"spiritual." Sometimes I say I am a life coach, which sounds vague but
legitimate, even corporate.

People sometimes are surprised that I segued from books to healing. I have
always felt that books are healing in themselves, and when I was at the bookstore,
often people requested a book for a sick friend or a bereaved widow. It was always
exciting to match the customer with the book that would be perfect for them and
perhaps transform their life in some way.

My sister Lucinda came across a program called Healing Touch, which
turned out to be a perfect complement to Buddhism in my effort to become someone who could help others. There have been a number of articles recently about
the plasticity of the brain and how one can learn to change one's way of thinking. I
had been helped tremendously by analysis, but I still had a ways to go. Sometimes,
if one talks or thinks too much about a negative experience, the neural pathway to
that memory can get wider and wider, making that memory even more likely to
recur in the future.

Now I was learning to heal myself by working in the energy field that surrounds the body. I like Healing Touch because it has a standardized curriculum and is widely available in mainstream settings, including Greenwich Hospital, where I worked for three years as a volunteer. (Alex loved my white nurse shoes.) It is a collection of techniques developed by different healers, ranging from Hopi Indians to a Christian minister, and collected by Janet Mentgen. It promotes healing and reduction of pain. Many scientific studies testify to the benefits of Healing Touch. The nursing profession embraced it in hospice care, pediatrics, and intensive care units. It is now associated with the American Holistic Nurses Association, so some treatments may be covered by insurance. Healing Touch, which was founded by Mentgen in the '70s, is now available all over the U.S. and in thirty-four countries around the world.

Healing Touch does not "cure," but attempts to make a person whole in body, mind, and spirit. Practitioners use their hands in a heart-centered way to support the client and promote healing. They work mainly in the energy field, or aura, that surrounds the body, focusing on the chakras, or energy centers, and restoring balance and harmony. A person's energy-body collects thoughts and feelings, and Healing Touch releases endorphins to the brain, increases circulation, and promotes a feeling of calm to aid the healing process. Through my practice of Healing Touch, I have learned to occasionally see a person's aura or energy-body. When I work with my clients I sometimes see shadows around their faces, or their feet if they are lying on my massage table. With my hands I can feel a client's energy field and determine whether it's hot or cold, dense or smooth.

I began reading a lot of spiritual books, and I became fascinated by Hildegarde of Bingen, an incredible visionary and nun in the Middle Ages. She became extremely influential, visited by emperors, popes, and bishops. She left behind many writings on science, art, and religion. Her music is still performed and widely regarded. One of my favorite sayings of hers is: "The body lives in the soul: not the soul in the body." Here is her drawing of the body in the soul or aura:

When I started taking private clients for Healing Touch sessions, I worked with problems ranging from pain to depression to insomnia. I set up my massage table in my bedroom, and before my clients arrived I lit a candle and said a prayer. Before I started I took some deep breaths and asked for guidance, so I could help my client heal. This is called "centering." After that, the client lay on the table, and I performed whatever treatment seemed most appropriate. Even though I found

Hildegarde of Bingen's drawing of an aura

it awkward to charge a fee, I knew I could never take myself seriously as a professional unless I did. It also turned out that the clients took my work more seriously when they paid. The payment became part of an energy exchange between us.

I volunteered for the Integrative Care Program in Greenwich because I wanted to do Healing Touch in a hospital setting. One morning I was knocking on doors on the sixth floor to see if anyone wanted to try Healing Touch. I entered a room where a conservative-looking Greenwich businessman was lying in the hospital bed, with his wife sitting by his side. I stumblingly explained Healing Touch to this totally skeptical patient, who was obviously in a lot of pain. After he emphatically said he was NOT interested, his wife encouraged him to try. He grudgingly agreed, and I did some Healing Touch techniques. Within five minutes he had relaxed and gone to sleep. I finished the treatment and started tiptoeing out of the room, at which point he woke up and said accusingly, "You're not LEAVING me, are you?"

The idea that I could help people who were suffering was a great source of joy. When I centered myself during the sessions, a sense of calm and peace swept over me. Both the client and I experienced the same healing benefits.

In retrospect, I think my study of Buddhism and Healing Touch was a way of learning how I could become happier and more at peace with myself. Psychoanalysis had been extremely helpful, but I wanted a more spiritual dimension in my life. Aristotle said, "We are what we repeatedly do. Excellence is not an act but a habit." My depression was a habit that became more entrenched as I grew older, despite medication, psychoanalysis, and other therapies.

I started reading the work of William James (brother of Henry and Alice), who, at Harvard in the late nineteenth century, taught the first psychology course in America. He believed each person had a soul that existed in a spiritual universe and influenced the way a person behaved. "The greatest discovery of my generation is that a human being can alter his life by altering his attitudes of mind," he said. "Be not afraid of life. Believe that life is worth living and your belief will help create the fact." This was very similar to what I had learned and practiced through Healing Touch.

A great source of comfort to me at the time was the Thursday Group. This group had been started by Margot Wilkie and her friend and sister-in-law Anne Morrow Lindbergh in the mid-1950s to ask a question no other women's social groups were asking: "Why are we here?" The early members included writers, an explorer, and others, numbering around fifteen in all. I was privileged to join around the time my bookstore closed in 1997.

We used to meet at each other's homes for prayer, meditation, and discussion of books such as Saint Augustine's *Confessions*, Huston Smith's *The World's Religions*, and Shantideva's *A Guide to the Bodhisattva Way of Life*. Later, we had an old-fashioned tea, with little sandwiches and cookies, and talked about our lives. We served as a support group for each other.

I remember once being so devastated over some family crisis that, when I arrived at the Thursday tea, I couldn't stop weeping. Barbara Ascher, a dear friend, and our hostess that day, had me lie down on her couch and covered me with a blanket. All the ladies sat around me and encouraged me, and I felt enveloped in a cocoon of affection! Margot was particularly good at dealing with one's emergencies; she stayed calm and nonjudgmental, no matter what. Then I would think, "If Margot doesn't take this seriously, maybe it's not so bad!"

Margot Wilkie (photo by Alex Sanger)

Margot Wilkie was one of the most amazing women I have ever known: her wisdom, humor, and nonjudgmental affection nourished her many friends of all ages. She grew up in a magical world, with remarkable loving parents. Her parents were great poetry lovers, and Margot enjoyed meeting their poet friends. Walter de la Mare even dedicated a poem to her.

When Margot was a little girl, and her mother was supervising construction on the family house in Martha's Vineyard, suddenly a little elf appeared. The elf grabbed the mother's leg and shook his tiny fist, saying, "All the elves are angry with you for disturbing us." Margot's mother responded by telling him not to worry, as this was all the work she was planning to do: the rest of the property would be preserved for the elves. At one point I said to Margot, "I love the story about the elf!" She replied, "It's not a story. It's true!"

Margot attended Radcliffe College, where she became the girlfriend of Lincoln Kirstein, who was the true passion of her life. She pursued acting and later started the Brattleboro Summer Theatre in Vermont with Constance Morrow, one of her dearest friends. Margot lived to be 101. She had two husbands, three children, grandchildren, and great-grandchildren. She made a serious study of Eastern religions and was a devout Buddhist.

Margot was so much more than I can convey: elegant, worldly, intuitive, humorous, devout, and fun-loving. I miss her almost every day and feel she was my spiritual mother, given her nonjudgmental love and support. After I completed my Healing Touch program, she was the first to ask me to give her a session.

At her 101st birthday party—looking gorgeous in pink—she gave a piece of advice to all the celebrants: "Forgive yourselves: just forgive yourselves..."

I read about a course in shamanism offered by Alberto Villoldo, a Cuban-born psychologist who teaches ancient Incan healing techniques. I enrolled in a course in his school, The Four Winds—Healing the Light Body, so I could dig deeper into shamanism. We learned ceremony and ritual for the soul, now often lacking from our daily lives. It was a rigorous program with seven-week-long classes held mainly at the Omega Institute in upstate New York that began on Sunday afternoon, continuing until the following Friday. We started at 8:30 a.m. and often continued until 10 p.m. or even later.

As in Healing Touch, we worked in the luminous energy field that surrounds the body: an information field that holds a record of past traumas and future possibilities. I remember experiencing this phenomenon while working on a client: I could feel lots of heat around her jaw, so I asked if she had any pain. She said no, but reported to me the next day that she had an inflamed tooth.

During some of our trainings, Peruvian shamans in colorful dress would appear and assist in our ceremonies and rituals. We'd break into groups, select partners (shades of dancing-class anxiety!), and practice on each other the techniques we were learning. Afterwards we discussed our findings with the group. I began to feel a bit confused and slightly guilty—was I a Buddhist or a shaman? My teacher Lama Yeshe said not to worry: they were both ways for accessing ancient wisdom.

During one of my week-long classes, we met for our final fire ceremony on a cold rainy night. We arrived by the fire, and our instructor selected one of the students and then asked him to remove his shoes and socks: I inwardly groaned, knowing I would have to do the same. She then made a small fire and instructed him to walk on it.

As we chanted, he did so with no pain or burning. When it was my turn, I danced on the flames and felt a sense of exhilaration and power. Now, anytime a task seems insurmountable, I remind myself that I was able to dance on flames

During another training session at a fire ceremony, I was surprised to see one of our shamans in the circle, as I had been told they weren't with us that week. The next morning I mentioned this to my group, and they all said none of our shamans had been there. I am still thinking about this and what the meaning might be... It was strange and mysterious, but not frightening, as I looked on the shaman as a powerful healer and a force for good.

One of the most profound classes I took was called "Dying Consciously," designed to help all people involved in the dying process—the individual, family members, and hospice workers—using techniques taken from ancient traditions. Among other things, we learned how to lift up the luminous energy field, or aura, from the body. We broke into groups of five and enacted my death: the other people were surrogates for Alex and my three children. Somehow the surrogates said exactly what my real family members would have said. I remember weeping and hugging the pretend Alex, saying, "I don't want to go." My energy field was lifted off my body, and suddenly I experienced a peace and joy unlike any other. When my group was calling me back, I didn't want to leave that peaceful place. This experience has changed my feelings about death, and I am no longer so afraid of it.

Just looking at things in a different way can change the outcome. For instance, when I was growing up I felt powerless and thought of myself as a victim. In fact, we all have an inner wisdom. If we choose *not* to listen to it, we end up living in confusion and unhappiness, instead of our natural state of joy. Now that I am often in the role of healer, I realize that the best I can do is support people as they help themselves.

All the great spiritual teachers, including Marianne Williamson, Jean Houston, and Gary Zukav, point out that there are basically only two emotions: love and fear. Fear can only lead to other negative emotions, such as jealously, anger, and depression. When your intentions are loving, you will be working from a higher level of consciousness and will feel positive emotions, such as affection, love, joy, and compassion.

At my final training at Omega Institute, the thought entered my mind that I should physically move to another apartment to tie in all the mental changes I had been making. Immediately another voice in my head said, "No, you can't move. You have to stay there 'til you die." So many of our teachings seemed to be about shedding whatever doesn't serve you and drawing in a new future. The more I thought about it, the more I realized that our apartment on Gracie Square, where

Alex, Jeannette, Matt, Ralph, and Andrew

I lived for forty years, no longer served my life. It had been a great place to raise our three boys, but now it was just the two of us and our cats.

By the time I arrived home I was utterly convinced that moving was the right thing to do. Poor Alex had just arrived home on the red-eye from Latin America and only wanted to fall into bed. He liked the idea of moving, and said that, if we were moving, we should move to a different part of the city. By the time he woke up, I had hired a real estate agent and was ready to begin our search. We had loved being near Carl Schurz Park and having a river view, so we looked for some place close to a park. Things seemed to fall magically into place, as though the universe was blessing our decision. Within three days, we had found an apartment overlooking Madison Square Park and sold our old one. As we were moving to a smaller apartment, we gave away and sold many of our possessions. It felt good to get rid of the accumulated stuff from the last forty years.

Our new apartment has a very different look than our old one. Its double-height windows flood the apartment with light. We have a bit less room but a more spacious feeling, because of the scale. No knickknacks, I decreed, even though my mother said, "Knickknacks make the room." No curtains: let the light in! We aimed for an Art Deco feel with minimal furniture. Our dining-room nook became El Morocco, with a zebra-patterned banquette. Soft colors and few photos prevailed. Sometimes the apartment as a whole feels like a very nice hotel where I can be completely in the moment.

We love our neighborhood, with the Flatiron Building advancing towards us like a stately ocean liner. The surrounding architecture, with its detail and history, fascinates us, and we are endeavoring to learn more about the architects that worked in our neighborhood. Unlike the static Upper East Side, our area is very lively, twenty-four hours a day, with many hip-looking young people with tattoos heading out as Alex and I are coming home. I am happy to be near the house Edith Wharton grew up in, as well as a lovely park where Henry James used to stroll; the same park was part of Herman Melville's route to his job as a customs inspector. In my mind all their ghosts linger there.

More and more, I am learning to look at things from a different perspective. I am creating a habit of happiness. In my work as a healer, I keep learning new techniques to help my clients. I've become a big believer in Laughing Yoga, for example, along with many doctors who have discovered the healing benefits of laughter. I took a course and am now a "Certified Laughter Leader." (My father would be horrified!) Absorbing the tenets of Buddhism and shamanism has helped break the bonds of my depression.

When I awake each morning, before turning on the computer, I light the candles in my healing room and say my Buddhist prayers and shaman prayers. I have altars dedicated to each practice. Then, in the peaceful candlelit room, I do my meditation: a practice that has helped me not be quite so attached to my own suffering (tempting as it is!). I feel it is my job to be happy each day: as happy as I can be, for myself and others. I always joke that I have to work about an hour each day to get where Alex is naturally—Lama Yeshe said he is "Buddhist by nature." Alex wakes up happy most days and is constantly thinking of others. For me it is more of a training with prayer, meditation, dance, singing, Laughing Yoga, and inspirational books all being part of the process. The volunteer work I do with my sister Helen in the emergency room of Lenox Hill Hospital helps give me a sense of purpose; the same is true for doing Laughing Yoga with the elderly (some younger than I am). I also value being on the board of the New York Society Library and the Open Center.

According to Buddhism, nothing is solid, not our bodies or anything else. As my teacher, Lama Yeshe, says, we are nothing but a bag of bones—and even bones aren't solid. Later on, science started to back up this theory. Instead of the physical

DAILY NEWS NYDailyNews.com
26 Wednesday, December 11, 2013
DAILY NEWS NYDailyNews.com

BIG TOWN **BIG HEART**

Gut buster

Laughter yoga helps veterans heal

Jeannette Watson Sanger (left) is a laughing yoga facilitator who works with veterans through Volunteers of America-Greater New York in the Bronx.

BY HOLLY REICH
NEW YORK DAILY NEWS

When Volunteers of America-Greater New York (VOA-GNY) was looking for something different to add to their roster of programs for veterans, laughing yoga topped the list.

"Jeannette Watson Sanger, the laughing yoga facilitator and volunteer, is the perfect combination of a professional who is skilled at her craft and has a genuine interest in working with veterans," says Rachel Weinstein, a vice president at VOA-GNY. "Her class is both engaging and restorative, and we are all quite pleased to have her work with us."

With more than 600 units of transitional and supportive housing, VOA-GNY is the largest provider of residential services for veterans in NYC. The first laughing yoga class was launched in September at VOA's veteran's residence in Manhattan, a facility that houses 174 vets, mostly men.

Yoga and laughter may not be the first thing that comes to mind when thinking of services for veterans, but Sanger says they are one of the most engaged groups she has ever worked with.

"We don't take ourselves too seriously," she says. "Laughing yoga is a unique exercise routine that combines group laughter exercises interspersed with breathing, stretching and rhythmic clapping. It fosters happiness and clears negativity."

Sanger claims that ten minutes of laughing yoga is equivalent to 20 minutes of jogging and an hour class uses up to 400 calories.

"It is very healthy — laughing engages 85% of your lungs," she says. "In classes we make a commitment to joy. The idea is to fake it 'til you make it!"

Sanger, whose brother-in-law was killed in the Vietnam War, feels strongly that giving back through her bi-monthly laughing yoga class is a special way to volunteer and help.

"These veterans have been through so much stress. The problem is that they come back from serving and many vets don't get a lot of support from the community. They aren't being cared for," Sanger says. "I have seen that even a half-hour yoga session is enough to alleviate some of their anxiety and trauma."

Relearning how to integrate back into society can start with the more basic pleasures of life — like smiling and laughing. Her participants report that they feel more optimistic, peaceful and calm after sessions.

Sanger notes, "One of the men said he couldn't even remember what he was worried about when we started, and another said he felt more relaxed. One veteran quoted some research — laughter produces chemicals in the brain that make you feel better."

Each session concludes with the vets telling their stories and sharing jokes. At the end of each session, Sanger leads a meditation and selects some prose to read. One of her favorite quotes by E.E. Cummings sums up her work: "The most wasted of all days is one without laughter."

In October, VOA-GNY expanded its veterans outreach as a grantee of the U.S. Department of Veterans Affairs' Supportive Services for Veteran Families. Through the program, VOA-GNY works to ensure housing for veterans and their families who are homeless or at imminent risk of homelessness.

Once eligible families are identified, case managers work with them to obtain benefits, secure referrals and access other services in VOA-GNY's continuum of care. Its services comprise the organization's largest veteran outreach to date.

For more information about VOA-GNY's veterans services, contact the Vets Helpline at (855) 2000-VOA.

For more information about volunteering, visit voa-gny.org.
holly@hollywrite.com

universe as described by Newton, scientists began to believe that everything is composed of atoms—spinning vortexes of energy within each individual. When I was reading about this, I was struck by the fact that, scientists report, the very act of observing something will change that thing. According to some healers and scientists, the observer, just by observing, is creating the new reality.

Do our thoughts create our reality?

I recently was discussing our childhood with my sister Helen, and she reminded me about how we used to levitate our friends and other sisters. This is what we did: One of the sisters would lie on the floor, with two other sisters on either side holding two fingers of each hand under the reclining one. I, as the eldest, sat at the head of the person lying down, with my fingers on either side of the head. Then I intoned solemnly, "She looks sick," which would be repeated by the other four, with great conviction, each time I spoke. Next, I would say "She looks dead," and "She is dead"; these statements were followed by, "She looks light," and "She is light," and then, "Let's pick her up." We only used two fingers each, but effortlessly and miraculously, the body would float up in the air about four feet, at which point we would lower it back down. I didn't think much about it, but now I wonder if I could do it again. Was it another example of the power of thought?

When I decided to become a healer, it opened my life in a new direction, and I was able to sense reality in a different way. By working with my hands in people's energy fields, I could sense heat or cold or congestion around painful areas. Sometimes my intuition guided me in techniques that could help my clients. Another time, my intuition surprised me: I had been encouraging a friend to reconnect with her parents, to whom she hadn't spoken in several years. I had a dream in which I was sitting with her parents, and my friend came to speak to them. I was somewhat freaked out when she called me excitedly on the day after my dream to report that she had just called her parents and made plans to get together. I am hoping to further develop my intuition.

When I decided to start writing this memoir, I had changed the way I viewed my past and saw everything, myself included, through a more compassionate lens. I felt I was becoming the hero of my life and not the victim of it. Sometimes I feel like Amos in William Steig's *Amos and Boris*: "One night, in a phosphorescent sea, he marveled at the sight of some whales spouting luminous water; and later, lying on the deck of his little boat gazing at the immense, starry sky, the tiny mouse Amos, a little speck of a living thing in the vast living universe, felt thoroughly akin to it all. Overwhelmed by the beauty and mystery of everything, he rolled over and over and right off the deck of his boat and into the sea."

Coming up for air, I find myself echoing Colette in saying: "What a wonderful life I've had. I only wish I'd realized it sooner!"

Acknowledgments

First: to my wonderful, patient, and brilliant publisher and editor, Ruth Greenstein.

To Stephen Graham Smith for his thoughtful editing.

For my darling Joyce Ravid, who took many of the photos in this book plus designed my beautiful cover.

To the following friends and family who offered to read my book and who gave me encouragement, advice, and support, I give my eternal thanks, appreciation, and love:

Danielle Araujo
Erite Araujo
Steven M. L. Aronson
Barbara Lazear Ascher
Angela Baggetta
Amanda Brainerd
Stephanie Cabot
Carey Cameron
Susan Cheever
Constance Christopher

Nicholas Christopher
Joan Hardy Clark
Todd Colby
Prudy Colsman-Freyberger
Helen Cook
Ann Marie Cushing
Clara Dale
Rowena Danziger
Jacqueline Weld Drake
Lewis Frumkes

Molly Haskell

Wendy Gimbel

Helene Golay

Lynn Goldberg

Brad Gooch

Angeline Goreau

Joy Harris

David Hopkins

Helen Houghton

David Johnston

Tom Jones

Bicky Kellner

Fran Kiernan

Phil Kovacevich

Kevin Kwan

Fran Lebowitz

Min Jin Lee

Nan Lee

Rebekah Lee

Pam Loxton

Ralph McElvenny

Daphne Merkin

Lance Morrow

Susan Brind Morrow

Susan Nagel

Lynn Nesbit

Peter Philbrook

Paul Raushenbush

David Sangalli

Alex Sanger

Andrew Sanger

Emily Sanger

Matt Sanger

Betty Kelly Sargent

Elizabeth Schmitz

Lisa Schubert

Susan Scott

Betsy Sweet

Lynne Tillman

Karen Tompkins

Lily Tuck

Patti Vaccano

William Villafranco

Patty Volk

Lucinda Watson

Margaret Watson

Olive Watson

Tom Watson

Deborah Weisgall

Susan Whitman

Throop Wilder

David Wilson

Jody Zara